THE ROCK'N'ROLL CIRCUS

First published in North America in 1978 by
A & W VISUAL LIBRARY, 95 Madison Avenue,
New York, New York 10016.

Library of Congress Catalog Card Number: 77-87150

ISBN: 0-89104-091-9   (paperback)
        0-89104-088-9   (hardcover)

Manufactured in Italy

Published by Arrangement with Pierrot Publishing Limited,
17 Oakley Road, London N1 3LL England

Rock'n'Roll Circus

THE ILLUSTRATED ROCK CONCERT

by Mick Farren & George Snow

CONTENTS

WAS ON A FLIGHT from New York, La Guardia, to Cleveland. My assignment was to watch the antics of a David Bowie tour. It was at what's become known as his 'Young Americans' stage of development.

The weather was lousy and the plane was rocking enough to spill drinks and reduce a good percentage of the passengers to abject, seat - arm - clutching anxiety. It's funny how, in this kind of situation, the passengers start talking to each other. I suppose it's the desire to make a final human contact before you drop out of the sky.

I was travelling this leg of the journey on my own. The guy sitting next to me was pretty much a standard model US corporate executive, or at least that's what I thought. The conversation opened with an exchange of comments on the roughness of the flight. According to the guy next to me, the turbulence on this particular flight was nothing compared to the one he'd taken from Boston to New York a few days earlier. That had been a real bad one.

For a while we both swapped travellers' tales and told appalling lies about ordeals we'd suffered in airliners. It started to sound as though the guy sitting next to me spent half his life in the air. I asked him what he did.

'I work for Ringling Brothers.'

'The circus?'

'Right.'

'What do you do there?'

'I'm an executive in charge of transportation.'

'You deal with moving the show from one place to the next?'

'Something like that.'

I told him that I was loosely connected with the rock and roll business. For the next twenty minutes we compared and contrasted the circus and rock and roll, while the plane lurched and bumped its way into Cleveland.

Although my companion was polite, and pleasantly attentive to my side of the story, he obviously looked on rock and roll as a small time operation compared with the problems of keeping a circus on the road. It was all summed up in one of his remarks.

Little Richard

'After all, when you have to deal with moving elephants, everything else seems kind of simple.'

Nobody in the rock and roll business would ever admit to anything being simple. Probably rock's greatest strength and also its major weakness, is that it takes itself very, very seriously.

The reason why rock and roll exhibits this single-minded self-regard almost certainly stems from its early days, and the way that a section of the population came on with such violent reactions to the music in its primitive form.

Rock and roll would have amounted to little more than another dance craze if its originators, Elvis Presley, Little Richard, Bill Haley et al., hadn't struck such a resonant chord in the basic human response. It was the Eisenhower, cold war fifties, a decade when human response was being suppressed about as much as it was possible for authority to suppress it.

The young took up the music as though it was the battle flag of freedom. The older generation, on the flip side of the coin, reacted to it as though it was both the devil's

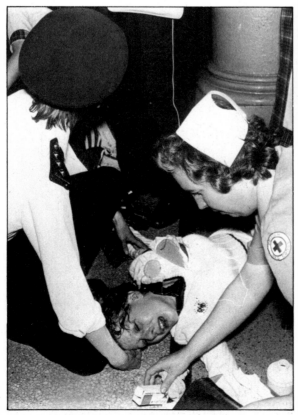

'Unplumbed delights or a sinister disruptive power.'

music straight from the jungle, and a subliminal trigger for mass juvenile delinquency.

With this kind of attendance on its birth, it was almost impossible for rock to see itself as just another musical form. Right from the start, the world treated it as something much bigger, either a source of unplumbed delights or a sinister disruptive power.

Things have hardly changed today. A British police chief in charge of a section of the outer London suburbs recently went on record with the opinion that 'drug pushers, pornographers and pop groups' were the main causes of the decay in modern society.

If society at large is going to credit rock and roll with such vast potential, the rock business itself is hardly likely to tell it any different. Something more than just a musical

Vietnam was the first war that was fought against a background of rock & roll from a transistor radio.

form produces a hell of a lot more money. Just how much a hell of a lot amounts to was estimated by rock impresario Bill Graham.

'In 1976, bicentennial year, it looks as though live rock music grossed more than sport in the USA.' Nothing that grosses more than sport can be very easily dismissed. Maybe keeping rock rolling isn't really so much easier than transporting elephants.

There have been a great many books that have traced the story of rock and roll. Depending on which one you read, it all started with Elvis Presley, Robert Johnson or African drumming. They usually wind up with a hope for the future. Again you have a choice. It can be Bob Marley, Mike Oldfield, Abba or the Sex Pistols who are the future of the music, depending on who's making the prophecy.

In the same way, the lives of the stars have been fully, if not overly, documented. What hasn't been anything but superficially investigated is the energy, the people and the technology that keep the music coming at us.

We may have heard the intimate details of the stars' sex lives, but few outside those directly involved really know the feel and smell of a rock concert or a recording studio, or realise what it takes to mount a tour or get an album into your neighbourhood record store.

In many ways, rock and roll does resemble the traditional circus. It certainly

Chuck Berry
Pic: JOE STEVENS

has its clowns, its high wire acts and its sweating roustabouts. It moves across the face of the planet with shambling precision. It has its hucksters, hustlers and barkers, although they frequently work out of an air conditioned office rather than a canvas tent.

Rock and roll has its animals, its camp following girls, its stars and its broken down has-beens. It's more common these days for a kid to run away to rock and roll than to join the circus. Like the circus, it has enjoyed spectacular nights of success and had appalling disasters.

It even has its geeks and grotesques who lurk in the shadows of the physical world and in the minds of performers and fans.

What it has the most in common with the circus is that the rock industry creates illusion and fantasy and sells it to anyone with the price of admission.

When the illusions and fantasies spread out over half the world and get close to monopolising its radio; when its followers take them to war with them in Vietnam and into the thick of student riots; when the same followers get to the point of believing that they may be the power that can regenerate an ailing society, and then become bitterly disappointed when they find out that illusions don't regenerate anything; then it all needs investigating. Maybe it's time to examine the energy and the people who keep the rock and roll circus on the move■

NOTICE
STOP
Help Save The Youth of America
DON'T BUY NEGRO RECORDS

(If you don't want to serve negroes in your place of business then do not have negro records on your juke box or listen to negro records on the radio.)

The screaming, idiotic words, and savage music of these records are undermining the morals of our white youth in America.

Call the advertisers of the radio stations that play this type of music and complain to them!

Don't Let Your Children Buy, or Listen

To These Negro Records

Fifties Ku Klux Klan anti-rock poster

The above scene from a fifties rock concert shows the influence of the natives' tom-tom on White Anglo Saxon Youth.

Pic: STEVE SPARKES

A sign on the endless trigway

Welcome
Bienvenue
Willkommen

Travel
Service

Welcome to Britain

Internal
Traffic Only

Way Out
A4 (M25. M3)

Way Out
M4 (M1)

Uxbridge A 408
Staines B 379
Hayes
The West
Slough   London
M 4   M 4

BADGER

George Snow

THE ROAD is the hard, hard core of rock and roll. It can turn a novice into a star and reduce an old hand into an abject mental wreck. It's sure as hell a lot more than a concrete ribbon between two points on a map; it's what live rock and roll is really all about.

The idea of going on the road again can produce a whole range of responses from musicians. Some view the idea with wide-eyed eagerness, others with weary horror. In the drunken small hours, veterans of rock tours talk about them in the way their fathers talk about the campaigns of World War II.

The methods and means of going out on the road are just about as diverse as the attitudes to doing it. At one end of the scale there are the Rolling Stones and Led Zeppelins in their rented 707s. At the other end there's the unknown foursome nursing a dying truck with a knocking engine and a set of bald tyres. On the surface, it would be impossible to recognise that each extreme really belongs to the same profession, or even in the same world.

Strangely though, they do. The superstar winners, the unknown hopefuls and the losers in between are all on the road, taking their music out to a paying public. Whether it's Joe Dink or Mick Jagger, they are all subject to the same basic set of worries and pressures, and experience the same peaks of excitement and gratification.

Of course, the degrees vary and so do the rewards. It's essentially money that produces the superficial differences. It's also money that can cushion the performer against some of the strains but, at the same time, money brings along its own set of problems.

No amount of money can change the fact that every working rock and roller is living the same basic life. It's a life that involves spending twenty-three hours of the day alternately building up and winding down from the single exhilarating hour on stage. Without that one hour, the road would be an impossible nightmare of absurd travelling, horrific hours, missed sleep and long stretches of crushing boredom. It's only the thrill of

Memorabilia of the rock stars touring youth — one day to be shown to bored 21st century kids.

that one hour in the spotlight that makes any of it worth while.

When the performer loses track of the excitement of the show, he's come to the point where he either quits or becomes yet another rock and roll casualty on the road. John Lennon summed up that state of mind in the song 'Cold Turkey'. 'Feel so suicidal I even hate my rock and roll' just about said it all.

Whether it's a two-lane blacktop or an eight-lane super highway, the foundation of the road is a simple problem of logistics. A bunch of musicians plus their sound gear and instruments have to be shipped between one date and the next.

The unknowns have it the simplest of all. They can get by with equipment that'll squeeze into a one ton panel truck along with the band. The stage crew usually consists of one scarcely paid driver/road manager. Finance isn't too complex either. The main fiscal problems are getting the petrol money to make it to the next town, deciding whether to get drunk and sleep in the truck or check into a fleabag hotel, and keeping one jump ahead of the payments on the equipment.

Further up the success ladder the operation becomes more complex. As audiences grow, the equipment load gets heavier, the road crew multiplies and the problems escalate. Just to get the Led Zeppelin from Kennedy airport to Madison Square Garden required three limousines and an escort of police cars and motorcycle cops. A visiting president couldn't have expected such care and protection. Visiting presidents aren't, of course, usually confronted by several thousands of fans who'd happily tear off their arm to take home as a souvenir.

In the realm of 30,000 plus audiences, equipment set-up and transportation gets into the pyramid building league. Techno-rock heroes Emerson, Lake and Palmer need three of the largest sized, twelve wheel semi-trucks to move the mountain of electronics that makes up their stage gear. It averages one truckload for each musician in the band to make himself heard.

Showco, the leading US staging and sound operation, provided the stage set for Bad Company's July 1977 concert at London's Earls Court exhibition hall. It required an entire 707 jet freighter to fly the

Equipment crew at work.
Pic: STEVE SPARKES

necessary hardware across the Atlantic.

It becomes almost impossible to believe that variations on the same function can alternately pack into a small truck or fill up a jumbo jet. And yet it's all basically the road.

When compared with the human beings, however, the problems of moving equipment are simplicity itself. Equipment doesn't wander off, overdose, get drunk, catch the clap, have nervous breakdowns or find itself thrown in a jail.

More than once, road managers have wistfully wondered why the members of the band couldn't be packed up in custom-made carrying cases, just like their guitars. When he's not on stage, the touring musician is little more than a spare part. Except in the poorest of bands, demarcation is rigid. The musicians do little or nothing to assist with the setting up or transportation. Coupled with this, the strain of psyching themselves up for the nightly performance, offset against the boredom of the rest of the time, results in a kind of naughty schoolboy attitude in a large number of bands on the road.

This is the attitude that causes bouts of hotel room wrecking, TV sets being dropped out of windows, drug happy rampages through the illegal pharmacopoeia and nightly sexual marathons.

You only have to look at the average day on the road to realise how easily outrage can break out.

The day usually starts around ten or eleven when the tour manager rouses and assembles his unwilling charges and attempts to corral them so they won't sneak off to the bar or otherwise get lost or mislaid. Once the band's been successfully herded together it's time to get into the cars or bus and begin the day's journey, either to the airport or the overland haul to the next city and the next stop on the tour.

There's only a limited number of ways to pass the time, either on an intercity flight or a long car journey. There are books and magazines, of course, conversation, gambling, set piece horseplay, drinking, getting stoned or simply going back to sleep. After the first few days of a tour, none of these are really sufficient to keep the minds of a group of possibly mismatched and probably hyperactive young men from becoming acutely aware that they're cramped, bored and cocooned in a private capsule, away from the normal world.

It's an environment that easily lends itself to abrasiveness, arguments, friction, paranoia and morbid introspection.

The first move at the other end of the journey is to check into the hotel. Few hotels offer any real novelty. The event of standardised hotel chains has created a situation where it's only the letterhead on the stationery that distinguishes a Holiday Inn in Amsterdam from one in Cleveland, Ohio.

It's ironic that only at the top and bottom of the success scale does hotel accommodation have any individual character. Each cheap motel or European bed and breakfast has individuality. So do the top flight, five star Dorchesters and Plazas. In between, there's rarely anything but a faceless standard pattern.

The late afternoon sound check is the first time the band have any part to play in the operation. It's the first chance for them to look at the stage and feel out the acoustics of the hall. With the gear set up they run through some of the show until the sound man's confident that the mikes and backline amplifiers are balanced.

Between the sound check and show time, the band is once again left to its own devices. The options aren't wide. They can hang around the hall or dressing rooms. They

Led Zeppelin's private jet

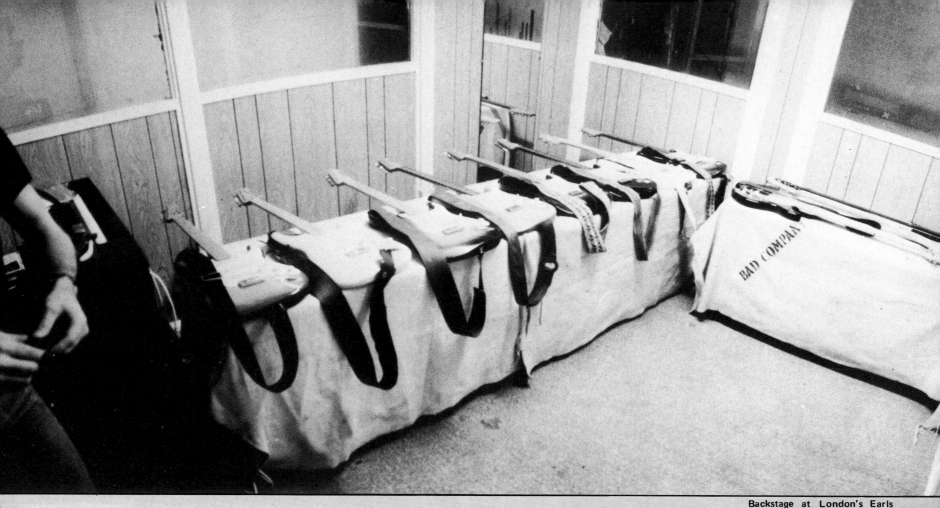

can go back to the hotel, grab a sandwich and watch TV. Even television can become another piece of stone tedium. The times when a musician is likely to turn on a hotel TV set coincide with the times that most TV stations put out their worst garbage — the afternoon soap operas and quiz shows and the early evening children's programmes. Afterwards all there is left is the late movies, if that. Bad television is just another of the small irritations of touring.

As it gets closer to the time for the band to go on stage, the musicians start to come into their own. They're no longer alternately tolerated and fussed over. This is their moment. They are the total focus of attention of all the crew, who are concentrating on getting them onto the stage, and of course of the audience itself. This is the whole frantic high point of the day. It's the only time when the music comes to the forefront. It is, after all, what the whole endeavour is about. It's the magical time of light, heat, sweat and noise that makes the boredom and irritation worth while.

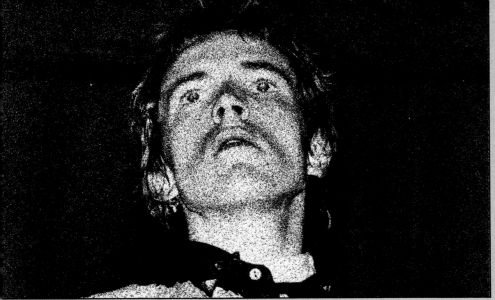

Johnny Rotten of the notorious Sex Pistols brought menace back to the watered down FM rock scene.

HOLLYWOOD STREET REVIVAL & DANCE

"BANNED FROM THE ROXY"

New York Dolls

GTO'S
IGGY POP, FLO & EDDIE, HOLLYWOOD STARS,
MICHAEL de BARRES, ZOLAR X, KIM FOWLEY,
RODNEY BINGENHEIMER, SURPRISE GUESTS;
POP STAR PIE FIGHT, FULL BAR & DANCING.
FRIDAY, OCT. 11 - 8 PM HOLLYWOOD PALLADIUM
ADVANCE TICKETS $5.50 AVAILABLE AT ALL
WALLICH'S STORES, LIBERTY AND MUTUAL AGENCIES AND
ALL TICKETRON OUTLETS

The New York Dolls (*above*) with their outrageous guitarist, Johnny Thunders (*right*) were early failures of Malcolm MacLaren but by 1976 he had got the formula right with Johnny Rotten and the Sex Pistols.

Different bands have different methods for winding down after a show. Some retire to their hotels, others go on the rampage. Not all bands, even when they can afford the damage bills, go in for the wholesale hotel destruction that's become the hallmark of Who and Led Zeppelin tours. (Keith Moon's damage bills reduced his takehome share of the profits from the last Who US tour to a mere £73.00.)

The temptation is always there, however, to prolong the excitement of the show and stave off the eventual anticlimax of the music being over and the realisation that there's yet another night to get through.

Getting through the night can become obsessive. In some bands it takes the form of almost unthinking groupie chasing; others cruise nightclubs in the endless search for drugs. Sometimes it all falls into place, and the night ends in one of the great parties that go down in the folk legends of the particular band. Other times it degenerates into the kind of gloom that hangs over sailors on shore leave who didn't score.

Even without the overwhelming desire to go out and look for action, the after-gig party would still get under way. For the musicians each city may only be another stop on the endless highway, but for the fans in any particular town it's a big night. Their heroes are in town; the more popular the band, the larger the number of local hipsters who want to talk their way into the hotel to party and hang out.

Eventually the night ends. There may be three, four or five hours' sleep before the next morning's call. Then the process starts all over again.

The first few days of a tour can be fairly invigorating. That's while novelty still holds good. By the tenth or fifteenth gig though, it starts to seem like a treadmill. Towns blur, faces begin to all look the same, and it feels as though the process will never stop. The musician pictures himself locked in a time warp of cars, hotels and dressing rooms from which there is no escape. It's the time when the phrase 'endless highway' stops being a self-glorifying joke and turns into a grim hallucination.

Far into a tour is when problems start. In some bands it's fist fights; in others, it's long, paranoia inducing silences. Hotel wrecking appears as a needed relief against real or imagined tensions. The severe deficit in the band's sleep starts to make speed or cocaine look like the ultimate necessity. It's hardly surprising that only a very few bands who are touring all the time fail to develop intraband superstitions and irrational fears.

At the end of the sixties a fear grew up between a number of English club and campus level bands about how many hours one could stay on the road in an overloaded and badly serviced truck without a major, fatal accident.

At the other end of the scale rumours circulated about how Mick Jagger was becoming obsessive about the possibility of being assassinated on stage by some crank. Meredith Hunter, the gun wielding black who was cut down by the Hell's Angels at Altamont, proved that the idea wasn't just road craziness but a real possibility.

Road craziness is basically a product of warped perspectives. A band on tour becomes such an enclosed unit that tiny things, without a tangible background to provide a sane context, get blown totally out of proportion.

The road may be hard but it's only hard within its own frame of reference. Veteran Nashville guitarist Charlie Daniels brings it back into focus.

'I get mad when these pussy-mouthed mothers tells me how hard it is on the road. The road's only hard because they drink too much, take too many drugs and don't sleep enough. They want to try pushing a plough across a field, following a mule's ass across a field for eight hours a day. That's hard.' ■

THERE'S A FASCINATION IN DEALING WITH LARGE NUMBERS OF PEOPLE...

Bill Graham

Jefferson Airplane in early incarnation

IF YOU ASKED the average rock fan in the street to name a leading rock and roll businessman, a lot of them would probably mention Colonel Tom Parker. Others would almost certainly say Bill Graham. Graham is something of a living legend in the rock industry. He is that unique combination of show-man and fiscal wizard that elevates the non-performer from a faceless backroom manipulator into a quasi-star.

In fact, it's hardly fair to call Graham a non-performer. Through his fourteen or so years in rock and roll he has often been in and out of the spotlight. He has introduced bands from the stage, publicly fought with them and fought for them. He has repeatedly clashed with the press, particularly *Rolling Stone*, and at one point he stood virtually alone, an easy target for the radical crazies who decided rock and roll should be totally free.

In a lot of ways Graham has been almost single-handedly responsible for the style of rock presentation over the past eleven years. He's one of the few promoters who has never been content just to go with the flow and bank the money. This need constantly to strive for excellence and continually innovate has made him a lot of friends and an equal number of enemies.

To understand Bill Graham and his work you have to delve into his background. He's a slim, wiry individual of medium height. He radiates nervous energy and a sense of theatre. His mannerisms are flamboyantly tense, rather like a street punk who finds himself grown up and successful. At times he reminds you of Lenny Bruce in his prime.

Originally, the young Bill Graham left a course in business studies to try for a career in acting.

'I got bitten by the acting bug. I thought I was the new John Garfield or the new James Dean, just like any other struggling actor.'

The acting career was not to be, however.

'I ended up in San Francisco as regional manager for the 3M corporation, then I ran across this insane theatre company doing things in the park. This was the San Francisco Mime Troupe. It was 1963. 3M was planning to transfer me back to New York. I had to decide whether I was going to stay with these crazy people or work towards being some sort

Leon Russell, veteran of a thousand open air rock concerts, seen here in summer plumage in his natural habitat.

The Band, Graham staged their farewell party, the 'Last Waltz'.

of successful executive.

'I decided I was good at business and not so good at acting but I could still stay in the theatre in some capacity. I joined the Mime Troupe as their business manager. I was called business manager, but in fact I did about everything, loading the truck, driving the truck, setting up the lights and carrying a spear when necessary. They were some of the best years of my life.

'It was during that period I met a lot of the San Francisco art underground. I had a loft and let this group use it to rehearse. They were called the Jefferson Airplane. I knew another band called the Warlocks who were later to change their name to the Grateful Dead. There were other people around, Frank Zappa, the Fugs. We ran into each other in the sewer, so to speak.

'In 1965 the Mime Troupe ran out of money and I had the idea of getting all the people together for a benefit. We could make a bit of money, and have a marvellous party. The first one was so successful that we had another one and another one.'

Graham hardly knew what he'd started. The benefit concerts began to overshadow the Mime Troupe.

'I started to look for a permanent place to hold these benefits and I discovered this old skating rink over in the Fillmore district.'

This was to become the original Fillmore auditorium. Along with Chet Helms' Avalon Ballroom, it was to grow into the rock and roll focus of the San Francisco magical period of 1966–67. Without really trying, Bill Graham had become one of the most important men in the new form of rock and roll that was mushrooming on the West Coast.

'I was an extremely lucky man to be in the right place at the right time.'

The Fillmore operation exploded out of all proportion. A second ballroom, Fillmore East, was opened in New York. The great bands of the era all passed across the two stages, the Who, the Doors, Jimi Hendrix, John Mayall, the Cream, Janis Joplin, Santana, the list was almost endless.

One of the things that made the Fillmores so successful was Graham's constant attention to detail. Everything from the posters to the lights and the security was pushed to the ultimate limits of creativity.

'I like to think that at the Fillmore, we were involved in improving the standards of the industry. Not just making a lot of money

Funky fans freak out at the free festival, Hyde Park, London (summer 1969) where the Stones played to 20,000 fans and 400 hot dog vendors. Mick Jagger's dress upstaged the lady on the right.

but introducing a lot of acts to the predominantly white audience we had. I don't say we discovered any individual, but if we were able to expose a Chuck Berry or a B.B. King or a Miles Davis or the Staples Singers to people who'd never seen them before, it was all worth while.'

Graham's high ideals found themselves under pressure during the late sixties. The Fillmores had stopped being a freaky experiment and turned into big business. Bill Graham was forced to move with it.

'I was constantly shuttling from coast to coast. I'd be in New York, say, the Friday and Saturday shows and in San Francisco for the Sunday night one. I made thirty-nine round trips in one year.'

Apart from getting jet happy, other problems came with success. 1968—69 were the peak years of anti-war protest, and political crazies latched on to Graham as an example of the arch capitalist exploiting the people's music. He became the bad guy in every would-be rock and roll Che Guevara's movie.

'It was as though they expected me to apologise for being successful.'

The one thing that Graham didn't do was say he was sorry. He met the radicals head on. In New York he offered a group called the Motherfuckers free community nights and was always prepared to debate any opponent, on the stage, in front of the audience.

In the end it wasn't politics that closed the Fillmores. It was simply that rock and roll had outgrown them.

'A certain way of life started to phase out. People no longer came for the reasons I started these places. Originally the Fillmores were a kind of church of music where the kids came to meet with their peers, not just see a band playing music. I think Woodstock, despite all that's been said and written, was the start of a new mass production in rock and roll.'

Bill Graham moved with the times. The Fillmores closed, but the Graham organisation continued to grow. He had a virtual monopoly on Bay area large scale rock promotions and also staged top level nationwide tours, including ones by the Rolling Stones and Bob Dylan.

'It was the world's only industrial commune run by a dictator.'

Despite being America's top promoter, Bill Graham still feels nostalgic for the days when rock could be staged in 3,000 seat, intimate halls.

'If I can get a group to play in a 3,000 seat hall, I will, but if they say "You present us in a 20,000 seat theatre," I do it. I had the choice of going into 20,000 seaters or getting out of the business.

'Some groups, like the Grateful Dead, will play five days in a small place, but more often than not the group will play the big places because we've now become very much like any other large business that works on the age old industrial theory of supply and demand.

'You have to realise that even rock stars want to spend some time at home enjoying the luxuries that success brings. If a Mick Jagger or an Elton John finds that he can make as much money on one date in Madison Square Garden as in a dozen dates on the road, nine times out of ten they're going to do Madison Square Garden. They're only human, after all.'

Instead of simply being nostalgic for the old times, Graham translates the nostalgia into a constant struggle to present better and

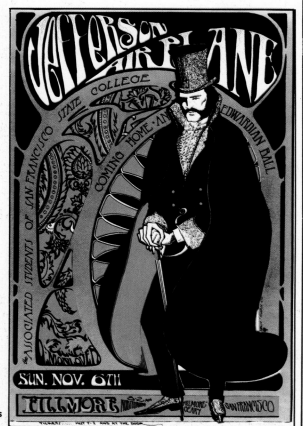

Fillmore posters from its psychedelic heyday

more original concerts. At a Peter Frampton show he decided to turn the stage into a Hollywood style medieval castle, but possibly his most ambitious project was the Band's final concert, The Last Waltz, where he not only had to get the Band and their guests, Bob Dylan, Van Morrison, Eric Clapton, Muddy Waters, Neil Diamond and Ronnie Hawkins on and off stage, but also coordinate feeding the 3,000 audience in the San Francisco opera house with a full Thanksgiving dinner and make it possible for Martin Scorsese to film the entire thing.

Graham's face takes on a look of delight when he recounts how he had to order ninety gallons of cranberry sauce as a single item.

Bill Graham could hardly be described as the typical rock promoter. While too many promoters' enjoyment simply comes from raking in the money, Graham obviously takes vast pleasure in presenting high quality rock theatre.

'There's a fascination in dealing with large numbers of people, and giving them a good time, that's like nothing else in the world.'

THEREV
-NOT CO
PRINCI

WERE 74 UNTING THE THE PALS

AS EARLY AS 1957, when Elvis Presley had rocketed to unprecedented fame, it became clear that rock and roll had grown too big to be contained in the places that held other musical entertainment. The kids who were flocking to the new music totally outstripped the capacity of the usual night clubs, ballrooms and concert halls.

In order to accommodate Presley's live shows, rock and roll promoters had to start thinking in terms of ballparks and open air arenas. From that time on the major league rock stars would start working in a unique world, with unprecedented sets of problems and challenges and exceptional opportunities to make money.

It was only nine years after the first massive Elvis Presley concerts that the question started to be asked: was it really safe to stage a major rock show without serious risk to both performers and audience?

Among the first people to pose that question were the Beatles. Their concert at Shea Stadium on their final 1966 tour of the USA showed such a potential for uncontrolled mayhem that it seriously contributed to the group's decision to bow out of the world of live performance.

The huge ballpark was packed to capacity with semi-hysterical fans in the grip of full-blown Beatlemania. Wire fences, crush-barriers and lines of police were fully extended to keep the crowd in the bleachers and off the central diamond where the stage had been erected.

The only safe way to get the Beatles on-stage was to drop them by helicopter directly in front of the stage immediately before they were due to play.

Even that was a close shave with disaster. The first glimpse of the superstars whipped up the hysteria to such a degree that one bunch of fans managed to break through both the barriers and the police.

Although extra police reinforcements were able to herd the fans back into the crowd, it did look, for a moment, as though they'd swarm over the band and the helicopter. Paul McCartney has recounted a flash of fear when he was absolutely certain that he

Pic: STEVE SPARKES

was going to be torn to pieces. He's reported as coming to the decision, there and then, that it was time the Beatles stopped performing in public.

The Beatles may have retired from the arena, but no amount of trouble was going to stop the progress of rock and roll. It was only a year later that a fresh experiment was being attempted in California.

Although few people realised it at the time, the Monterey pop festival was to set patterns for the presentation of rock that would last for the next five years.

Instead of the screaming, unpredictable frenzy of the crowd at a Beatles concert, the people at Monterey were stoned, enthusiastic but completely in control. They might want to freak out and do idiot dances but they didn't show any signs of wanting to tear the stars limb from limb and take home the bits as souvenirs. Even Brian Jones could move around the festival site without any problems.

Admittedly, the acts who appeared at Monterey weren't, at the time, in anything like the Beatles bracket. They did, however, put down such powerful performances that it spun Jimi Hendrix, the Who, Otis Redding and Janis Joplin straight into the international spotlight.

The success at Monterey seemed to point towards a newer, better way to present big name rock and roll in a safe and profitable context.

Through the next four years, rock festivals mushroomed all over Europe and the US. The people organising them were a varied lot: slick popbiz hustlers, well-meaning but inept entrepreneurs and sleazy used-car salesmen out for a quick buck.

Gradually people began to realise that the staging wasn't as simple as it first appeared. It was also clear that a rock festival, unless very carefully handled, wasn't the instant gold-mine it had initially been taken for.

Even before a festival got under way there was usually a good deal of hostile flak from the authorities and local residents, in the form of protest committees, petitions and court injunctions, to be dealt with. By 1970 the situation had become so fraught with this kind of difficulty that promoters started keeping the site of the event secret until the last possible moment.

From an audience of **50** at the Cavern Club, Liverpool to crowds of **50,000** at Shea Stadium, New York, the Beatles packed them in from Wigan to Wisconsin.

The hip-shaking youth from Memphis finally makes it to Heartbreak Hotel — Caesars Palace, Las Vegas.

anarchists, White Panthers and bike gangs banded together in organised attacks on the fences and pitched battles with security guards. By halfway through the second day of the three day event, the organisers were forced to declare the festival free.

After a few incidents of this kind, it became clear that a state of diminishing returns was setting in. The cost of the security needed to collect admission money was simply too high. By the mid-seventies, the staging of festivals was limited to small, free, hippie-organised celebrations. The money-men started to look for new ways of presenting top line music.

In the USA, the problem was solved for the rock promoter as vast multi-purpose entertainment complexes like the many Coliseums, Houston's Astrodome or the LA Dodger stadium were built. These new structures were capable of handling anything from circuses to sports events. They were also perfect, from at least the promoter's point of view, for staging giant rock and roll shows.

Europe, however, wasn't so lucky. Nobody seemed too willing to invest the necessary millions to provide entertainment centures for the final quarter of the twentieth century. European tours still had to find a home in less than suitable sports stadia like the Palais de Sport or London's Empire Pool, ramshackle conversions like the Pavilion de Paris (a derelict slaughterhouse) or acoustically dire exhibition halls like London's Earls Court.

Securing a site was only the start of the festival promoter's troubles. The quarter-of-a-million people that turned out for some of the biggest gatherings stretched any conceivable water, sanitation and food facilities to extreme limits. Woodstock was only turned from disaster to legend by a near miracle and a major helicopter airlift.

Had it not been for the returns from the movie, Woodstock would have been one of the biggest financial catastrophes in the history of rock. Other backers weren't so lucky.

By 1969 a new headache had been laid on the festival promoter. In the highly charged political atmosphere of the late sixties the cry for free music became very popular among sections of the audience.

At the 1970 Isle of Wight festival French

One of the results of this unsatisfactory situation in Europe was that it began to become, in rock terms, a poor relation of America. Bands like the Rolling Stones and the Led Zeppelin began to look on European tours as something approaching a charitable act. The USA emerged as the only place where the top-liners could make real money. Some of the big names continued to tour Europe, just hoping to break even. Others, like Bob Dylan, simply missed it out. The absence of suitable venues for the biggest rock names meant that Europe, for practical purposes, was simply non-viable.

Viability was very much the keyword of rock promotion during the second half of the seventies. From its hustling, haphazard beginnings it had evolved into a highly organised, intensely professional industry. Just how professional was proved on the Rolling Stones' 1975 tour of the USA. According to the released figures, the cost of the tour was somewhere in the region of ten million dollars. It grossed thirteen million, leaving the Stones with a neat three million profit.

From the giant, block-long billboard in Times Square that announced the tour, down to the lavish, full-colour programme, every detail was covered.

Aside from the normal load of sophisticated sound equipment, the Stones even went so far as to carry their own stage, a huge, elaborate, star-shaped construction complete with its built-in lights and a forty-foot inflatable phallus. The points of the star folded down from a vertical position at the beginning of the show. The effect was like the unfolding of some monster flower. As the petals opened, the band was revealed for the first time, plugged in and ready to boogie.

Apart from giving an impressive visual opening to their act, the design of the stage also ensured that any over-eager fans would have a very difficult time trying to make physical contact with the band. Rumours circulating around Los Angeles also suggested that the flaps were bullet-proof and, in the event of trouble, could be swiftly flipped up, completely enclosing the Stones and covering them from every side.

The Stones showed that they had learned the lesson of Altamont. There was no question of messing around with makeshift set-ups,

amateur help or Hell's Angel bodyguards. Each one of the seventy-three people was a top specialist. From the sweaty crew to the pilot of the private plane, everyone knew exactly what he was doing, and he did it. Even seemingly small details like the allocation of backstage passes and complimentary tickets can, on a tour of this size, amount to something like a full-time job.

Certainly the work that went into the tour more than paid off. The scene in the Los Angeles forum was little short of magnificent.

The folding stage, looking like a huge scale model of some futuristic cathedral, dominates the circular auditorium. As the forum usherettes in short orange tunics and white mid-sixties go-go boots show the audience to their seats, massed Mexican drummers keep up a furious tattoo from the base of the stage. Overhead, long Japanese silk banners swirl lazily in the air conditioned breeze.

A Rolling Stones concert has become something akin to a royal visit. As the crowd files into the auditorium heads crane to spot the celebrities. Ringo Starr and Elton John receive a standing ovation when they take their seats.

Backstage the society jostling is even more intense. In Los Angeles Raquel Welch, John Phillips, Olivia Newton-John, Charles Bronson and Liza Minnelli are among the fortunate few who receive passes to the VIP suite. In New York Bob Dylan dropped in, as did Santana. In Washington DC, Jack Ford, son of the then president, showed up with Andy Warhol.

Passes to the Stones' dressing area have become the modern equivalent of the social register.

Scenes and society are forgotten, however, when the lights go down. This is the moment that all the work, the precautions and the planning have been leading up to. This is why all the money has been spent and why the crowds have gathered.

The petals of the stage slowly unfold. Keith Richard is standing on one of them, kicking at it to make it open faster. It's a very human touch. Amid all the slightly unreal opulence, it's a comfortingly real note. He may be decked out in a lemon yellow suit, but underneath it all Richard is still impatient to rock and roll.

The planning doesn't end with the start of the show. The set is carefully paced to keep the audience's maximum attention. As Jagger puts it:

'The audience needs a curve with a slight lull in the middle, otherwise they wouldn't have the energy for the end of the set.'

But what about the Stones' energy?

'If I get exhausted, well — if I do, I adopt my Robert Plant stance with an imaginary tambourine. Actually it's a rather long show. I'm not used to it. Robert Plant and Jimmy (Page) have been able to do these long shows, and one of the reasons is that they have these 35 minute drum solos, in which they can go back to the dressing room and start a conversation, pick up a girl, have something to eat . . . and this is in the middle of the show.

'You see what I mean? The longer it gets, the crazier it gets. I could never see that before. We're doing two hours. We haven't done that since 1965. We used to do long shows then in ballrooms. We would do four three-quarter hour sets. We would do everything, anything, we could think of. Anything to fill up the space.'

The space is still adequately filled. Aside from the music, Jagger swings out over the audience on the end of a rope, he rides the giant phallus and a long Chinese dragon threads its way through the audience.

Despite the careful planning there's still tension at a Rolling Stones show. Nobody has forgotten the assassination attempt at Altamont. It's taken them five years to summon up the courage to play *Sympathy for the Devil* in public, after the disastrous effects that the song produced at the free concert. When they finally did attempt the song at a Madison Square Garden concert, a firecracker exploded. For a moment, everyone froze.

At the end of the show, mass psychology quickly has to reverse itself. Having spent the last three hours winding up the crowd, every effort has to be concentrated on cooling them out. Soothing orchestral music is played over the PA. Everything has to be defused before the audience stream out on to the streets. Repeated announcements make it very clear that the Rolling Stones have already left the building and that there is no point in hanging around for a final fleeting glimpse.

The 1975 Stones tour may have seemed, at the time, to be the peak of rock and roll

Robert Plant and Jimmy Page before the 40 minute drum solo. Pics: PENNIE SMITH

Kiss — grotesque marionettes
of glitter rock.

flamboyance. The subsequent years have proved this not to be the case. Top-line bands have gone to further and further extremes in elaborate effects and staging.

Peter Frampton appeared on a stage mocked up to look like Hollywood's impression of an English castle, complete with cannons and beefeaters. Kiss travel with what amounts to a full horror movie set which allows them to breathe fire, spit blood and set off thunder flashes and Roman candles with total gothic impact.

The major rock and roll show has hit such extremes that the word 'overkill' has started to be bandied about. Emerson, Lake and Palmer discovered that they had gone to such lengths on their 1977 US tour, with a seventy-piece orchestra, lasers and miniature hovercraft, that they were actually losing money.

The rock new wave is currently proclaiming that as far as they are concerned, this kind of lavish presentation will be a thing of the past in a couple of years. This is easy to say when most of the punk bands are scarcely out of the club stage. It will be interesting to see if, when they reach the big stadia, they'll be able to resist spending massive sums of money on special effects. Minimalism has a terrible tendency to melt away in the face of crowds of over thirty thousand■

"You can't always get what you want."
Pic: PENNIE SMITH

THE POVERTY TRAIL

DO YOU KNOW anywhere we can sleep tonight?' The hangers-on in the dressing room shake their heads. Nobody can come up with a place for the band to lay their heads. The bass player shrugs. 'Looks like its gonna be the van.' The place happens to be the Electric Circus, rock joint in Manchester, England. The band is called Motorhead and the time is early 1977. It hardly matters, though. It could be anywhere on earth where rock and roll is played, any band and any time in the last twenty years. This is the poverty trail, the absolute bottom line of rock and roll.

It's the network of tiny veins that feed live rock and roll out to the clubs, town halls, high school gyms, campus hops and National Guard armouries across the world. It doesn't matter if the back roads are in the American South or the factory towns of northern England, it's pretty much the same story, give or take a few local variations.

It's frequently wretched, always broke and too often desperate. It's fuelled on beer, take-away food, cheap whisky and cheaper bathtub amphetamines. Finding the money to keep going can be a nightmare. Usually the only tangible reward for the rock and roll band working at this level is the fact that it gets to play at all.

Not for them huge crews of sweating roadies, limousines, private jets and wall-to-wall groupies. At the bottom of the rock pile, the most help a band can expect is one driver/road manager, who's lucky to get paid, and maybe some kid who's just come along for the ride. The finances on the poverty trail are minimal. It's a matter of scraping together the gas money to get to the next gig, deciding whether to check into a motel or spend the money on getting drunk and sleep in the truck. If the truck or the equipment irrevocably break down it can spell disaster.

In the spring of 1977 Motorhead had been living like this for too long. It was no consolation to them that any number of the world's top stars had shared the same experience. It doesn't make you feel any better to remember that the Beatles slept in the verminous back room of a Hamburg cinema or that the Rolling Stones came close to starving in a run down Chelsea apartment. When you're on the poverty trail the only place you want to get is out — out of the scuffling for pennies and into the smart hotels and big time tours.

Lemmy, the bass player of the three-piece outfit, has had a couple of previous tastes of the better times. In the middle of the sixties he had a minor success with Liverpool's notorious Rockin' Vicars; later, during the flower power lunacy of 1967, he was involved in a less than successful raga/rock fusion unit with a sitar player named Sam Gopal. Some two years later he joined Hawkwind, the

Motorhead — "It's tough at the top, but it's tougher at the bottom."
Pic: MOTORCYCLE IRENE

anarchic British psychedelic band, where he enjoyed a couple of chart hits and the dubious privilege of trekking from one Holiday Inn to the next as the band repeatedly toured Europe and the US Midwest.

Following a minor drug bust at the US-Canadian border between Detroit and Ontario, Lemmy found himself fired from Hawkwind. The next project was Motorhead, a band of his own.

The original Motorhead line-up had some initial success, coasting on Lemmy's previous reputation. They were booked for a major London concert supporting Blue Oyster Cult.

It was promoted along the lines of a battle of the bands, the upstart American rockers against the homegrown British boys.

The competitive, gunfighter atmosphere was a bad miscalculation. The line-up wasn't gelling and the audience noticed. So did the critics. The band's reputation was irrevocably damaged. Gigs got harder to get, and the three original musicians showed no real signs of coming together. Soon there was nothing left but garbage gigs, and eventually the first stage of Motorhead went their separate ways.

Lemmy recruited two new sidemen. Guitarist Eddie Clarke had once played with

Curtis Knight, a black showman whose main claim to fame was that he at one time recruited the young Jimi Hendrix into his band.

Phil Taylor's origins are far less specific.

'I've been in a lot of garage bands, as they say.'

This cracks Lemmy up.

'He used to be in a band with a petrol pump.'

'Motorhead's the first band I've been in that's working — and not earning money. Before I joined I was really living. I had a permanent address and a car. I was doing fine, now look at me . . .'

Underneath the wisecracks there's a kind of grim hardness. The temptation to feel that the rest of the world is engaged in a conspiracy against them is always lurking around a band in this position.

'Nobody's paying for Motorhead to go into the studio.'

'Nobody's paying for Motorhead, period.'

'Nobody's paying for all the gear that's blown up tonight.'

'I mean, we need bread to repair the amps, and I've only got two pairs of sticks left, and one of those is odd.'

Sticks, blown amps, the next meal, a bag of speed or a six-pack of beer. To a band at the bottom of the ladder, these can be insurmountable problems. Mick Jagger may fret about a possible assassination, these boys worry about starving.

They also worry about their boots wearing out, about being dirty and down at heel, about the girlfriends who walk out because they've had enough of buying the groceries and staying home nights because there isn't any money to go out.

The worst feeling when you're down on this level is that the poverty will never stop. Too many bands on the back road circuit being to feel like the Flying Dutchmen of rock and roll, doomed to stay the same way for ever and never climb out of the rut.

Climbing out of the rut can be hard. In fact, it gets harder the longer a band stays on the poverty trail. The unpleasant truth is that without some injection of capital, it's ten times more difficult to get to a level where living becomes even a fraction above wretched.

All too often it's a heavy investment

rather than talent that impresses agents and promoters to take a chance on an unknown band. Even when there is someone picking up the tab for a bunch of beginners, they can still be unmercifully exploited. Playing support on a club date can cost a band hard cash. Once the trucking, PA hire and other incidentals have been deducted from the gig money, the result can frequently be a minus sum. The reality of this situation is that the band are actually paying to play.

It became clear that the paying to play syndrome had moved into a more advanced stage when a scandal erupted in the international rock tour business. The story was that certain unnamed first division bands were charging newcomers four figure sums for the honour of playing the opening spots on their tours. The rationale for this was simple. Opening on a major tour means optimum exposure. Exposure is something that is worth money, hence the four figure cover charge. All too often, this is the logic that controls the rock business.

In the case of a band like Motorhead, the rut climbing problem is more complex, probably by about a factor of ten. The first

Too much for too long, Lemmy catches up on a little sleep. Eddie Clarke (*right*) does more with his secondhand Telecaster than some musicians do with a brand new custom Les Paul. Phil Taylor (*left*) 'I'm only in it for the memory.'
Pics: MOTORCYCLE IRENE

strike against them was the failure of the original band. In addition to this they played hard uncompromising rock and-roll, had a reputation for wildness, drugs, and a tendency to hang out with speedfreaks, Hell's Angels and the local lowlife. It might look very romantic in a printed biography, but it made the business shy away from the band.

The second line-up was much more successful than the first. Successful, that is, in terms of the scattered audiences that they managed to play to. The kids may have grown to like the band, but the business hardly went along with them. Motorhead continued to scuffle for a living on the very edge of disintegration.

If anything, the situation was aggravated by the knowledge that it really was the rock and roll business, unwilling to let them live down their previous bad name, that was keeping them from, if not success, at the very least, survival.

The story probably would have ended there. Motorhead was on the verge of disbanding and calling it a day in the spring of 1977. For most bands on the poverty trail this would have been the point at which they let go their grip and sank into oblivion. But Motorhead suddenly stumbled across a stroke of luck. It's something that probably only happens to one band in twenty in their position.

The first part of this break was when they attracted the attention of Ted Carroll. Carroll ran a small London based record label called Chiswick. Previously Chiswick had specialised in releasing fairly obscure fifties rock material, but with the increase of the singles market in a depressed UK, Carroll had decided to expand into the field of a modern, if possibly off-beat, product.

He paid for Motorhead to record a single and then an album. At the same time, the second part of the break arrived. The band was offered the support spot on a Hawkwind tour of Britain. Although Hawkwind themselves weren't doing too well by this time, there were sufficient audiences to allow Motorhead to make their mark.

Their single managed to reach the lower end of the charts and the business, which had previously written off the band as hopeless losers, began to sit up and take notice. Motorhead was signed by a major management operation and, at least provisionally, their future held some better prospects than starvation and musical drudgery.

In a way, the story of Motorhead is a bit of a rock and roll fairy tale. Most of the bands who have been down that far, never manage to resurface. They simply stay down. Their future holds no promise at all. They can either go on playing their music and earning conspicuously less than an unskilled labourer, or they can give up.

Often the unknown band that remains that way doesn't do so because of a noticeable lack of talent. All too frequently it's because they haven't been in the right place at the right time, because they haven't been seen by the right people or because their image and material are out of step with what the holders of the purse-strings consider commercial.

It's ironic that rock music should provide some of its practitioners with millions of dollars and deny others even a minimal standard of living. For a music that has talked so glibly about equality and freedom, the inequalities in its own ranks can, at times, be glaring ∎

"This band takes no prisoners"
Pic: MOTORCYCLE IRENE

CAN YOU HEAR ME IN THE CANS?

JUST LIKE everything else in the world of rock and roll, the recording studio comes in every size from the humble to the lavish, one for every rung on the rock and roll success ladder. They range from small, hole in the corner places, little bigger than the average living room, with a single engineer nursing patched up equipment, to luxurious, live-in palaces like the Record Plant in Los Angeles, where the facilities for the after hours orgy are as spectacular as the recording equipment.

Ironically, the quality of music that's produced doesn't really go hand in hand with the opulence of the studio. Some of the great rock and roll classics, like Elvis Presley's Sun recordings and Buddy Holly's *Peggy Sue*, were cut on the most primitive equipment. Sam Phillips' studio in Memphis, Tennessee, and Norman Petty's studio in Lubbock, Texas, were as basic as you could get. Their recording machines were far less sophisticated than a present-day home tape-deck.

Sounds had to be created by ingenuity and improvisation rather than banks of electronic equipment. Echo was synthesised by the use of concrete sewer pipes, a packing case might be substituted for a bass drum to get the right percussion sound. It's a wry joke that it has proved close to impossible to reproduce accurately those early rock and roll sounds in modern studios with as much electronic hardware as a NASA control room.

Hunter/Ronson recording

The first ten years of rock and roll didn't see an awful lot of technical advance in the recording studio. Producers like Phil Spector, Shadow Morton, who was responsible for golden oldies like the Shangri Las' *Leader Of The Pack*, and Brian Wilson of the Beach Boys all radically changed the overall quality of the rock and roll record but, once, again, the changes were due to inspiration and ingenuity rather than great advances in the actual equipment.

Phil Spector's 'wall of sound' technique, that was such a part of the success of the Crystals, the Ronettes, the Righteous Brothers and Ike and Tina Turner, was almost wholly a result of orchestration, arrangements, studio acoustics, echo and a good deal of unique thinking. At his peak, Spector scorned using anything more complex than a simple two-track machine.

Even the Beatles at their most baroque, on the *Sergeant Pepper* album, worked on a four-track recording rig.

After *Sergeant Pepper*, however, all hell broke loose. Recording machinery took giant leaps. The four-track with its modest half-inch tape began to divide and grow like some sort of horror movie monster. Eight-track became the norm, then sixteen and finally twenty-four or thirty-two with massive two-inch tapes rolling at fifteen inches per second.

Recording costs also escalated. It wasn't uncommon for a top-line band to vanish into the studio for months on end. Occasionally, as in the case of Stevie Wonder's *Inner Visions*, the months could actually run into years as sound was layered on to sound an' remix followed remix to reach supposedly ultimate masterwork heights.

The album *Day at the Races* by Queen was just such a case. It was nearly a year in production and cost something in the region of half a million dollars.

The atmosphere in a recording studio naturally varies from band to band. Some are quietly tense, others are boisterous. Nonetheless there are certain elements that are common to every session. There's a sense of being part of something important. No matter how often you go into a studio, you can't help being impressed by the control room. The huge mixing desk is awesome. Dozens of coloured lights cast an eerie science

George Snow

David Bowie — 'Take 700!'

Brian Wilson — as his recordings became more complicated, they became less successful.

Andy Colquhoun of Warsaw Pakt adding his contribution to the first 'direct-to-disc' recording in Britain. The system involves live sound played directly on to the matrix for improved sound quality.
Pic: GERRY GORE

fiction glow. The control room of the average studio could easily be the bridge of a futuristic space cruiser about to warp into battle.

It's a fairly lax space cruiser, though. The recording industry doesn't suffer from the extreme overmanning that blights the movie studios. Even the largest studios frequently only employ an engineer, a tape jockey and maybe a studio assistant.

The studio itself is a complete contrast to the control room. This is where the musicians work in a clutter of instruments, leads, sound baffles, cigarette butts and empty beer cans. There is always, even in the most barnlike studio, the eerie deadness of a sound-proof room.

The techniques of recording have changed quite radically over the twenty odd years of rock and roll. In the early days a band would play live in the studio. About the only concession to the recording was to enclose the singer in an isolation booth to prevent the vocals being swamped by other instruments.

Today, it's a whole different ballgame. Although parts of the band may still play together, each instrument is recorded on a separate track. Vocals and extra effects also get tracks of their own. Once all the

Studios London boasts
s 32 input 24 output
plus Eventide Digital
Harmonizer and Phaser,
Expanders, Urei Gra-
qualizers, EMT Delay
tecs. The tape machines
24, 16 and 8 track and
ler A80 2 track. Clients
cluded Marvin Gaye,
, John Denver, Genesis,
1usic and Bob Marley.
IAN COOKE

components of the tune are down on sixteen (or however many) tracks, the lengthy and often trying process of mixing them down to a simple stereo tape begins.

Mixing is the most crucial part of modern recording. The master tape is run over and over again until the ideal balance between the voices and various instruments is achieved. Once everyone is satisfied that they have the best possible blend of sound, the final mix gets under way, and the song is reduced down to the more manageable stereo tape. It's from this tape that the end-product vinyl disc is eventually cut.

In recent years there has been something of a revolt against the over-lavish and super-expensive style of recording. The simultaneous rise of punk rock and the return of a singles orientated record buyer has led to a greater simplicity of production. Studio time has been cut back to days, over-dubbing cut to a minimum. It could be that the album considered as a Cecil B. De Mille epic is a leftover from 1960s craziness and will soon become a thing of the past.

On the other hand, the Rod Stewarts, Rolling Stones and Elton Johns who still seem to want to spend months creating forty minutes of music will probably keep the giant machines rolling for quite a few years to come.

Freddy Mercury of Queen, the group that comes second only to 10CC in the amount of tape used up in each session.
Pic: PENNIE SMITH

OLD LADIES
-ROAD LADIES AND

OH SHIT I FORGOT YOUR NAME

ISOMETIMES WATCH the faces musicians pull when they're on stage and wonder if they make the same faces when they're fucking.'

The lady, who didn't want to be named in print, grinned impishly. 'A lot of them do.'

I doubt there's anybody who would attempt to deny the very solid link between rock and roll and sex. Certainly no musician would, and neither would the girls who, at times, seem capable of moving heaven and earth to get close to the guitar picker of their dreams.

Indeed, if the truth were told, the initial impetus for a large percentage of today's rock stars to pick up an instrument was the hope of getting laid more.

Pete Townshend, always one of the more candid of rock's senior superstars, summed the whole thing up.

'When I was a kid I used to think the size of my nose made me so diabolically ugly that my only hope was to put a guitar between me and the rest of the world. I locked myself away for two years to learn how to play one.'

Eric Burden confirms the same idea.

'If most musicians owned up, they'd have to admit that the reason they first got into rock was because they thought they'd get to ball an awful lot of chicks.'

In fact it goes even deeper. In the twelve years that the Rolling Stones have been together as a band, Mick Jagger has almost single-handedly changed the ideal of male beauty. When the Stones first hit the road, it was still the era of Cary Grant, Steve McQueen and Yul Brynner. By contemporary standards Jagger was grotesque going on hideous. He had a slack wide mouth with disproportionate, rubbery lips, limp, unkempt hair and the kind of body that Charles Atlas got rich trying to put right by correspondence course. And yet he struck a vital chord in the sexual make-up of young women across half the world.

The force of his presence, coupled with teen female fantasy, transformed him in a few short years into an ideal of masculine cute. Just how much of an ideal is summed up by a lady who, in the late sixties, got herself tagged as a 'top New York groupie'.

'I screwed a lot of the top names at the

Linda Ronstadt — suckled on country pleasures.

time. I was hanging out at Steve Paul's Scene. It was the ultimate hip place in those days. Balling names was what it was all about. We used to compare notes afterwards. The girls, that is. You know what I mean? There was the famous phrase that used to get tossed about. "Yeah, so-and-so was great but he wasn't no Mick Jagger".

'Then I actually got to fuck Jagger and, Jesus Christ, all I could think of afterwards was that he was great, but he wasn't no Mick Jagger.

'It makes it all kind of dumb really, doesn't it?'

The late sixties, the days of the Fillmores, were the heydays of groupieism. Of course, rock and roll and sex went hand in hand before that, and continued to go hand in hand afterwards. The late sixties were, however, the time when groupies became a media cult. Many of them, working on the Warhol principle of everyone being famous for fifteen minutes, did their damndest to elevate themselves to the status of minor celebrities.

The most publicly bizarre had to be the

April — the costume department worked undertime, the girls worked overtime, but no-one worked on the sound.

Plaster Casters of Chicago. The Plaster Casters were a crew of dumpy, nondescript teenagers who made up for what they lacked in looks by outrageous notoriety. Their unique selling point was that they didn't just sleep with rock stars, but kept a permanent record of the liaison in the form of plaster casts of the musicians' genitals.

This unique art collection was sufficient to merit them a feature in *Rolling Stone* and a lengthy chapter in Frank Zappa's as yet unpublished *Groupie Papers*.

On the Hollywood Sunset Strip, the Plaster Casters found sisters beneath the sheets in the persons of the GTOs. At basics the GTOs were a self publicising, organised team of girls who fell in with the Frank Zappa operation, and even got to make a semi documentary album. This contained, as well as reported anecdotes and some bizarre songs, a recorded telephone conversation in which one of the ladies recounts how she attempted to preserve her virginity specially for guitarist Jimmy Page.

Even the sexually inhibited English made a contribution to the groupie legend. This was a novel, simply and directly called *Groupie*. Written by Jenny Fabian, this was a semi autobiographical account of the adventures of a lady who, after taking a job as box office girl at a London psychedelic club, finds herself spending a lot of her waking hours engaging in oral sex with a prodigious list of currently popular musicians.

When the book was published in 1968, it caused a great deal of amusement in the London rock scene, since in many chapters only the names had been changed to protect the not-so-innocent. The whole incident was brought closer to the boil when the infamous *Oz* magazine published a directory to the real individuals behind the pseudonyms.

Although, at the time, the idea of groupies was grabbed and sensationalised by the media as a further example of the depths that contemporary youth had sunk to in their degradation, the existence of rock and roll camp followers is very easy to understand. Like the drifter, the gambler and gypsy before him, the rock musician on the road comes into town with a ready made air of mystery. He comes from a different world, and is

Not all women in rock are confined to home or hotel. Labelle and the Runaways are among the ones who have made it to the performers' side of the footlights, while the Tubes lay out parodies of rock & roll excess.

invested with all the romantic excitement of the exotic and the unknown.

All this, coupled with the fact that the rock musician also puts on what amounts to an at least covert sexual display, leaves little doubt why teenage girls, (and older, for that matter), caught in a dreary routine of high school, shop counter or factory, should take him to their hearts and their beds.

What starts as a simple response can, however, turn into something sordid and destructive when it starts to move to neurotic extremes. When groupieism reached the point where the girls were prepared to fight tooth and painted nail for a seat in the star's limousine or a favoured position in the hotel room hierarchy, a very definite sickness set in.

Instead of a statement of sexual independence, the nightly post-concert fumblings turned into a desperate status race among the girls. It started to look as though being a serious groupie meant being prepared to take part in any kind of physical degradation thought up by sexually spoiled musicians. It was either that or be out of the game.

Both sides of the groupie syndrome

started to suffer. Dignity went out of the window, the men increasingly started to look like jaded, brutally sexist libertines and many of the girls got to be little more than dead eyes behind a painted cosmetic mask.

To complicate matters, more than just the musicians wanted to get in on the act. Roadies, security men and hangers-on all exploited the more than willing road ladies. The name of the game became 'If you want to ball the star, you've got to ball me first.' One stage door guard at New York's Fillmore East was fired after he'd boasted he could get as many blowjobs as he could handle. It was the price he charged for letting girls into the auditorium's backstage area.

Like so many of the excesses of the sixties, the groupie scene eventually burned itself out. The burn-out wasn't without casualties, though. Of the five GTOs, two are dead.

Although the groupie scene has faded, it doesn't mean that today's rock and rollers have taken to celibacy. There are still ladies around like the one at a recent Thin Lizzie concert in Texas who yelled out, loud and clear, how much she'd like to suck the dick of bass player Phil Lynott. The main difference

Through the seventies women have increasingly demanded an equal shot at rock fame. Reading left to right Natalie Cole, Patti Smith, Gaye Advert, Fanny, Lynsey de Paul, the Runaway Gloria Mundi, Crystal Gayle, Carole King, Goldie & the Gingerbreads, Blonde on Blonde, Dolly Parton and Tanya Tucker.
Gloria Mundi pic: NANDO VALVERDE Gaye Advert pic: STEVE SPARKES

between today's rock environment and that of eight to ten years ago is that it does seem that today's musicians and today's female hangers-on have learned to avoid some of the more wretched extremes.

Although the media might lead you to think otherwise, groupies aren't the only women involved in rock and roll. Large areas of rock administration are controlled by women. The top prestige jobs, though, are still, as in so many other industries, filled by men. There are dozens of lady publicists, public relations officers, artist liaison executives. Sadly, there are damn few women producers, A&R persons or company presidents.

The most difficult role for a woman in rock and roll, aside from perhaps attempting to beat the men at their own game and actually get on the stage and play, is that of the musicians' wives, old ladies and permanent girl friends. In a world as transitory and frantic as rock, long term relationships are far from easy to maintain. For the musician who is regularly touring, a family life requires constant thought and effort to keep it functioning.

Solutions to the problem can range from thoughtful and open minded agreements to self deluding hypocrisy.

One of the main stumbling blocks to long term relationships is, of course, the presence of other women on the road. Some musicians' wives take this threat in their stride. The wife of Country Joe McDonald was once quoted as saying:

'I'd rather my old man slept with the occasional chick on the road than tried to stay faithful to me and drove himself crazy. I don't want him sitting round in some hotel room, two thousand miles from home, feeling horny and feeling he can't do anything about it because of me.'

Not every rock and roll couple manages such an enlightened attitude to their relationship. One British musician and his wife maintained an elaborate and costly pretence each time he was away on an American tour.

Every night after the show, he'd place a call to his wife and spend up to fifty dollars in transatlantic toll charges in convincing her that he was remaining absolutely faithful. Once this duty was discharged he'd join the rest of the band in the nightly ritual of drug

George Snow

The Crystals "bad, but good bad, not evil"

taking and groupie chasing. Back at home his wife also went about her own affairs as and how she wanted.

The varieties of rock musicians' steady ladies are as many as the attitudes to the relationships. On one hand you have the Bianca Jaggers and Britt Eklands who have all but replaced the Taylors and Burtons in the gossip columns of the daily newspapers. On the other, there are the self-effacing home bodies who never make the papers and seem to remain in a traditional, almost secretive role of looking after the musician's country retreat, bringing up his children and generally behaving little differently from the women left behind when their lords and masters went off on the crusades. Possibly the only improvement is that rock stars have yet to discover the chastity belt ■

'What's a nice girl like you doing in a place like this?'
Pic: STEVE SPARKES

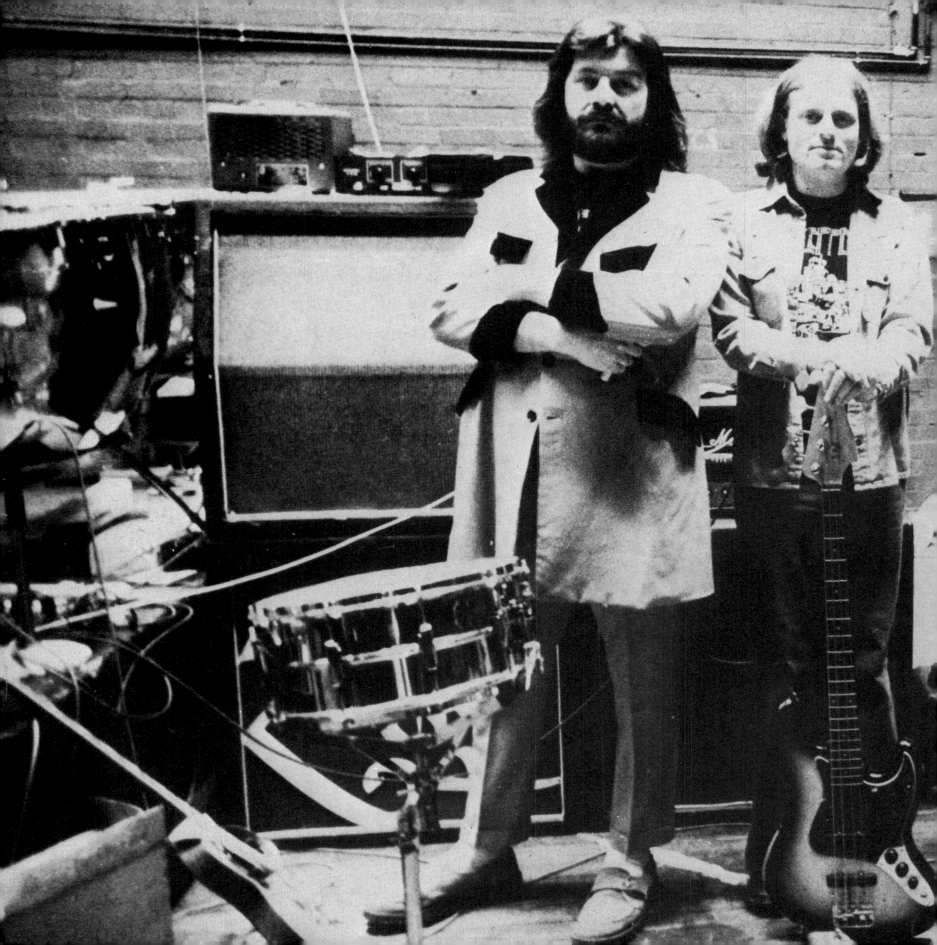

Pic: PENNIE SMITH

THE CIRCULATION IS USUALLY CIRCULAR

YOU'RE ALWAYS worst off in the middle. At least, that's what the musicians in the middle of the heap invariably tell you. The poor boys at the bottom of the heap may scrabble and starve, the gilded creatures at the top may wander the labyrinth of cocaine psychosis and million dollar tax bills but in the middle you just go round and round, constantly expending energy and usually getting nowhere.

This is the world of the bands who have managed to fight their way out of the horrors of the poverty trail. They work, they record. They have, to one degree or another, mastered their instruments. They enjoy a minimally decent standard of living. What usually wears them out is the knowledge that after maybe the second year of being in this position, they're stuck there. They become increasingly aware that they're doomed to remain for ever in the position of rock and roll also-rans.

The economics of this stratum are far less touch and go than on the poverty trail.

The cash, however, doesn't flow in the six or seven figure sums that support the excesses of the stars. The problem is that in order to maintain the degree of prestige to keep working, and to mount the lighting and sound equipment necessary to present an acceptable show, the band simply have to go on and on playing. The whole fiscal situation of this level of band is so close to the break even point that there's hardly ever any margin for expansion.

For them, the highway really does seem endless.

The stock in trade of this part of rock and roll is a two, three or four thousand seat auditorium. Their happy hunting grounds are the larger cities in Europe and the USA. Of these, the prime money making market is the American Midwest. Year in and year out, dozens of bands shuttle back and forth between Kansas City and Cleveland, Detroit and St. Louis. Beyond that there are the side trips to London, Paris, Hamburg, New York, Atlanta or Los Angeles. The lucky few even manage to evolve a following in Japan that allows the occasional visit to Tokyo. It's not

Ted Nugent — partially deaf in one ear (that'll larn him).

strictly what could be called a hard life, but beneath the hectic succession of one night stands there is an underlying frustration that somewhere the band has missed the bus.

In order to exist in the middle league of rock touring, the band have to keep up an operation that's often quite out of proportion to the cash returns they make from playing. They have to carry a vast PA, a sound engineer, an equipment crew that can often number as many as five or six.

In addition to this, there's the cost of trucking the equipment many thousands of miles a year, coach class air fares for the musicians, hotel bills, commissions to agents, percentages to managers and, last but by no means least, the band's own wages. Frequently these compare far from favourably with the take-home pay of an unskilled manual worker.

In order to make this basic nut, the absolute bare minimum break even income, the band may find itself working two hundred or more days in the year.

Although many musicians in this bracket may support a home, wife and even a family somewhere, their real home is the procession of Holiday Inns, Sheridan Motor Courts, Trust Houses, Novotels and Ramada Inns. Life on this stretch of the road may not be exactly wretched. There are compensations. The more a band tours, and the more times they return to the same towns, the more they are able to get a grip on some kind of reality. They at least have the chance to form relationships. The people they meet on the road cease to be simply hangers-on or one night, thankless gropings, and become genuine friends.

Despite all this, there's still a dangerous psychological undertow. The constant, rootless travelling still has a creeping, mind numbing effect. The dreams of stardom fade. The myths of overnight success have been very solidly proved to be nonsense. In moments of depression it can look as though the round of hotels and paint peeling dressing rooms will go on for ever. Band members start to remind each other that they're not getting any younger. Secretly they wonder if there's any way out at all. The musician in his late twenties or early thirties becomes very aware that his only saleable trade is playing the

Bob Seeger took almost ten years to find his niche in the rock hierarchy.
Pic: PETER VERNON

never get any further, there are a few who manage to break through to the next rung of the ladder. Thin Lizzy plugged away for some four years before they broke through to stardom. Similarly Aerosmith seemed doomed to circle the Midwest until they grew old and grey, and then suddenly, young America decided they might be the next Rolling Stones. It took Bob Seeger ten years to find international recognition. Steve Miller experienced a similar uphill grind.

Probably the most surprising character to break out of the non-stop touring circuit is the self styled 'Motor City Madman' Ted Nugent. Nugent had a minor hit during the psychedelic sixties with *Journey to the Centre of Your Mind*, a sensory overload guitar feedback epic. Nugent, however, failed to follow up that success, and lagged seriously behind the other Detroit bands like the MC5, the Stooges and Mitch Ryder and the Detroit Wheels.

What Ted Nugent did achieve was to carve himself a solid niche on the Midwest circuit. It started to look as though Nugent was doomed to churn out his brand of raw, ear-bleeding guitar for the American heartland.

'Those halls we played in the sixties. There was Billy Lee and the Rivieras (later Mitch Ryder) and the Supremes. At the start of the evening, people would be moving towards each other, by mid-evening they'd be touching each other. Then the band would work its way up to loudness and really blast everyone.'

Blast or not, there were times when the Nugent routine flagged. In order to boost audience response he resorted to shattering glasses with guitar high notes. Even this was a piece of fairground deception. More often than not a concealed roadie would administer the coup de grace with an air pistol. Another schtick was to engage in guitar duels with other down-on-hard-times Detroit pickers. Even on a Midwest tour where the audiences aren't exactly the most sophisticated on God's earth, this really constituted unashamed barrel scraping.

Towards the end of 1975, change seemed to take a hold on Nugent's fortunes. He signed with Columbia records and suddenly, without any major promotion, Nugent's sound was being demanded by a far wider audience than the Valium and wine kids of

guitar, the piano or the drums. He finds himself in the same dilemma as the black bluesmen of the past have been in all their lives.

The grind doesn't even stop with the end of each tour. In between times, the band have to squeeze in a fairly heavy recording schedule. The record companies are well aware that it's perfectly viable to issue regular albums by a group on this level. They may not be expensively produced or receive any high pressure promotion, but the record companies are aware that although the records aren't likely to rocket up the charts, the bands have sufficient following in the cities they play regularly to make the exercise a practical proposition.

As in everything else concerned with rock and roll, there are exceptions to every rule. Although by far the biggest percentage of bands on the small time touring circuit

the suburban Midwest. There was no doubt that he'd moved on and, at least for a couple of years, put the world of cut price touring behind him. He was on the front of magazines, headlining ten thousand seat concerts and unmistakeably going up.

There are many explanations for a phenomenon like Nugent's sudden success after so many years. Probably the only one that really holds water is that the rock audience, despite all attempts at analysis and prediction, is totally capricious.

Nugent himself has an answer that is completely in keeping with his loud macho style.

'The record company's finally hip to what's going on. They're just catching up to me. I never slow down. It's team work. Everybody's so competent now, and I trust them.'■

Ted Nugent is another musician who has spent a decade in the search for fame.

The Roadies
Get to Eat First!

ONE OF THE bad things about roadies and road crews is that they'll take any kind of shit you throw at them. Even the most tatty hippie is tied up in the idea that the show must go on. I guess the attraction of being a roadie is like the kind of thing that got cowboys off. You're always on the move. You never know where you're going to be tomorrow. You usually have quite a lot of cash in your pocket.

'There's a certain bravado in walking into a new town. It's also a very, very social job. You've got ten or twelve people on the crew, you see them maybe twenty hours a day. You're working very hard to put the gear up. You spend the time chatting and bull-shitting across the stage while you're working, farting around, playing silly games. There's also a lot of booze, a lot of drugs and a lot of women.

'In some cases it's paid quite well, while, in others, it isn't. The last cowboy image may seem silly, but it's also true. It's like the American truck driver. It's one of the last jobs with some kind of romance about it. The conditions can be really awful at times, but there's an amazing company loyalty among roadies, which is pretty surprising for a bunch of radical hippies.'

See Factor is a lighting operation that provides comprehensive lighting rigs and operators for the upper echelon touring bands. It was originally formed in New York, but as it grew and expanded, branches were established in Los Angeles and London. Paul Clements and Stephen Hurston are co-directors of the UK branch of the organisation.

When you talk to Clements, known to his friends as Clem, a lot of cliches spring to mind. It's very tempting to talk about 'unsung heroes' or 'the behind the scenes backbone of rock and roll'. The popular image of the roadie has, over the years, come to be that of a sweating oaf with more brawn than brains, beer can in one hand, a joint in his mouth, coaxing broken-down equipment back to life with fuse wire and gaffer tape while keeping an eye out for stray groupies.

In today's world of rock and roll, nothing could be further from the truth. Today's top level road manager is a highly experienced specialist. Clements explains:

'When heavy road rock and roll started it was like one in, all in. You helped with this and you did that and everyone gangbanged in. In the last few years it's become much more specialized and disciplined. It's also got so much bigger. You can't throw all the gear in the back of a transit any more. It's semi-trucks all the way, and it takes three or four guys to put up just one part of the gear. You really have to be a specialist in your own field.

'There's a lot of advanced technology in rock and roll today, a lot of people working in rock and roll. If you're going to function properly you have to know something about a whole range of subjects, electricity, electronics, welding, stress factors, how to hang things, trucking, the best routes to use, the best places to stay. It's turned into a pretty complex job.'

One of See Factor's major clients is Richie Blackmore's Rainbow. When Rainbow go out on the road their equipment load can be pretty formidable.

'They use three semi-trucks, one full of lighting, one of sound equipment and one mixed. There are a crew of four on the lights, maybe four or five on the sound and four more with the band.'

As well as Rainbow, See Factor has worked with Aerosmith, Ted Nugent, Blue Oyster Cult, Patti Smith, Deep Purple and Bob Dylan. The UK office figures to be able to handle four tours at once, and this is only Europe, which is very much considered the poor relation of rock and roll. Lacking both suitable halls and facilities, and with national borders hampering movement and complicating administrative work, the European rock tour is forced into a much smaller context than its US counterpart.

'When a band like, say, Aerosmith goes on tour in the USA, it's a question of a hundred to two hundred lights. In Europe we're talking in terms of seventy or eighty.'

The contract equipment business is highly competitive. A top-line band will be satisfied with nothing but the best.

'A major act will put out bids for a lighting system. If they have their own lighting designer with specific ideas he designs the rig he wants for the band. He takes a compromise between the best price and whoever is offering the closest equipment to what he wants.

Clem
Pics: ROBIN SCHWARTZ

'Some bands who don't have a lighting designer come to us for the design plus the equipment and the crew. Then it's entirely up to the guy working for us.'

The relationship between roadies and musicians can vary between the democratic and the downright feudal.

'Some bands won't let you near their dressing room. Some walk on a knife-edge to such an extent that they think you'll destroy their charisma. Others would rather have your company. You just walk in and help yourself to a beer from the band's barrel. If they ask what you're doing you tell them, "We're nicking your fucking beer, ain't we?" '

One of the most unusual jobs handled by Clem and See Factor was Bob Dylan's Rolling Thunder Revue.

'It was a magical mystery tour for the first part of it because they refused to tell anyone where they were going. That pissed me off intensely because I still maintain there's life beyond rock and roll. I had the rent to pay and didn't know where I was going to be day to day. I didn't like that bit, but aside from that it was quite different from any other tour.

'They didn't promote the tour. They didn't tell anyone it was coming until two days before. They carried their own ticketing, security, the entire production.

'They took out an option on every suitable hall in New England, and exercised the option on a particular hall three days before they wanted it.

'The first gig we did was in Plymouth, Mass., in a tiny municipal hall that held just 1,500 people. A lot of the crowd were extremely sceptical as to whether they were really going to see Bob Dylan, and Joan, and Joni Mitchell, but they did. It riveted them in their seats. It was the quietest audience I've ever seen. They were stunned.

'It was the only tour I've ever done where I watched every show. It was a revue. At most rock and roll shows, you have the tedious opening act for 25 minutes, half an hour, while they wally around on the stage pulling the drums off. Then there's the tedious second opener, and after that you've got to wait 45 minutes while they clear the stage for the main act. You're dog-tired and you want to go home. You're not really sure if you still like the band any more. You have

to sit through their hour and a half. It's only then that you can go home.

'With Rolling Thunder everyone played on the same stage, through the same gear, and it just flowed. Although it was five hours long it didn't interrupt at all. One person would come on, another would go off. It was an ideal format for rock and roll. For me, it was the best tour.

'It was also about the only tour I've done where there was almost total segregation between the workers and the rest, which we didn't like too much, being the workers.

'There were 105 people on the road with the tour. Only 15 were crew, about 10 were concerned with administration, 20 were musicians and all the rest were free-loaders.'

One example of the problems this creates was the matter of food.

'When you do a double show, it's traditional that you eat between shows. The first in line, no questions asked, are the roadies, because they've got to eat and get back to get everything together for the next show.

'We'd go to eat and have to wait while forty-five dildos munched their way through all the food.

'We staged a doughnut strike somewhere in Massachusetts. We refused to work until our coffee and doughnuts turned up. They didn't arrive until about 2.30 and we'd been there since eleven. It put the show back by about an hour.

'It was one of the few cases of industrial action on the road.' ■

Pills, ills and a

Pic: JOE STEVENS

shot in the dark.

George Snow

Let It Rock

"THE WORLD'S BEST ROCK READ"

Buddy Holly
1936-59

Sam Cooke
1937-64

Otis Redding
1941-67

Brian Jones
1942-69

Jimi Hendrix
1943-70

Janis Joplin
1943-70

IS THERE ROCK AFTER DEATH?

British fan mag Let It Rock presents rock's book of martyrs

Buddy Holly — the original living dead. Others rushed to emulate his success.

DO WE REALLY have to rake over the ashes of past disasters one more time? There have been periods when the rock media have seemed to take an almost necrophiliac glee in sifting through the minutest details of a star's suicide or a concert that wound up being a massacre. There are always those who can't resist pontificating, agonising or, worst of all, the ones who jump in with both feet, grabbing a fleeting, centre-stage spotlight by claiming to be the victim's closest friend, the only one who understood.

As most other worlds, rock and roll is liberally sprinkled with its ghouls. Not only the ones who want to grab public attention, but the less ambitious vultures and vampires, the ones who cluck and tut and discreetly gloat over any tragedy.

I suppose in such a youth-orientated industry as rock it's hardly surprising that the death of a musician is always accompanied by ripples of severe shock. Youth is not a time for thinking about dying, unless it's in grand, dramatic terms. This has produced a tendency to over dramatise the various casualties that the music has thrown up over its two decades of life. Similar factors have also caused a definite inclination to group together all the musicians whose deaths terminated their careers into some kind of spurious Rock and Roll Book of Martyrs.

The British fan magazine *Let It Rock* actually went so far as to produce such a work. Almost the whole of one of their issues was devoted to a day by day calendar that marked the demise of just about anyone who had the loosest connection with rock and roll. In some cases, the connection was pretty damn loose. Leon Trotsky, James Dean and Sonny Boy Williamson were all included in this rock roll of honour.

This sort of morbid iconography has clouded the real causes behind the deaths of rock's most celebrated corpses. There is no real, legitimate link between, say, Buddy Holly's death in an air crash and Jimi Hendrix's overdose. Any connection between Morrison floating dead in his bath in a Paris apartment, and Brian Jones floating face down in his English swimming pool, has to be

GEORGE SNOW

Iggy Pop (nee Stooge, nee James Osterberg)

at least tenuous. Anyone who wants to draw a parallel between Johnny Ace blowing himself away in a backstage game of Russian roulette and Sam Cooke being murdered by a hooker has to be weird in a very convoluted way. Two of the Allman Brothers may have been killed in motorcycle accidents, but the idea of sinister, metaphysical implications is scarcely a rational one.

Looking for an overall connection between the various casualties of rock tends to blind one to the real truth that every individual who, one way or another, broke down under the strain of being a performer was a unique case. To think any other way is to deny the humanity of that particular performer.

The early rock disasters were, in the main, accidental. Plane crashes claimed Buddy Holly, Ritchie Valens, the Big Bopper and later, Otis Redding and Jim Croce. Auto wrecks took out Eddie Cochran, Johnny Kidd and quite a few others. The list may stretch out, but it should hardly surprise anyone. When you consider the huge number of man hours that rock musicians spend on the road, a whole lot of transit deaths are only to be expected.

If any form of disaster has to be seen as particularly applicable to rock and roll, then I guess you have to pick on the kind that are drug related. There's no denying that far too many musicians have gone out in either

A fan's shrine to James Dean

The Ford Mustang belonging to Bay City Roller Les McKeown after he had hit and killed a 75 year old woman pedestrian

eith Richard: a constant
urce of fan speculation
c: CHALKIE DAVIES

desperate or just plain stupid overdoses.

The narcotic explosion of the sixties claimed more than its fair share of victims. The paisley, mind altering flood that swept across the USA and Europe threw up its dead with a vengeance.

Even before the event of rock, drugs had claimed victims among musicians. Hank Williams had died of a heart attack after consistently popping too much speed to keep him on the road. Charlie Parker succumbed to bleeding ulcers, the result of a lethal diet of booze and heroin.

The illegal or semi-legal pharmacopeia has always offered a chemical solution to the musician's problems. Whether it's too much fame, too much money, too many disappointments or simply too many towns in too few days, there's always a pill or a powder that'll ease the pain.

There are two main categories of drug that rock musicians fall prey to. To be brutally simple, it's usually either uppers or downers that cause the trouble. Of the two, the uppers, primarily cocaine, amphetamines and amphetamine substitutes like Ritalin, are the less harmful of the two. The uppers, the stable diet of the overworked band on the run, may cause physical deterioration after prolonged use, and psychological problems in the short term, but do not have the sinister record of fatal overdoses that surround the downer group.

Downers, which range from heroin and morphine through the various forms of barbiturates, Valium and the Quaalude/Mandrax methaqualone group, present the most serious chemical danger to the working rock and roller. The main problem with every form of downer is that in the morning small hours of a rock tour, they're so damned attractive.

The whole family of downers, to one degree or another, offer the musician a warm, comforting cocoon which temporarily protects him against everything from the stresses of the road to the often unreal strains of sudden stardom.

Whether it's in a hotel bar, after a show, when the hangers on are getting too much to stand, or simply when a young performer finds him- or herself abruptly pitchforked into a world of big money and high pressure business, it can be all too pleasantly tempting to insulate the mind with either barbiturates, heroin or one of the others.

All types of downers are readily available in the world of rock and roll, as, for that matter, are most other drugs. To complicate matters further, a dealer who becomes a major act's main supplier of downers is on to a free ride into the comforts of upper crust rock excess. It's a very major incentive for any hustler to promote his product seriously.

If any individual wants to keep his mind in comfortable insulation, it should be entirely his own affair. The trouble starts when all downers produce an escalating physical tolerance. In order to maintain the cocoon, he has to take more and more pills. Once the consumption of, say, Quaaludes goes beyond handfuls of half a dozen or so, the obvious temptation is to switch to the much more efficacious heroin.

The theory of escalation from marijuana to heroin has been pretty well proved to be nonsense. Unfortunately a similar link between barbiturates and heroin is a little too real.

Once the brain has reached the point where it's swallowing handfuls of this, snorting up lines of that and even injecting some of the other to keep away reality, the temptation comes to do away with reality altogether. The line between a careless overdose and a deliberate suicide is thin and blurred in the mind of the terminal downer freak. The large number of rock stars whose deaths were connected in some way with downers bears appalling testimony to this.

The list is awesome. It includes Jimi Hendrix, Janis Joplin, Al Wilson, Paul Kossoff, Frankie Lyman, Florence Ballard and Billy Murcia of the New York Dolls.

If you class booze as another form of down drug, the list becomes even longer and more frightening. You have to add names like Jim Morrison and Gene Vincent.

The tie-up between drugs and rock and roll causes other disasters than deaths through overdose. Even the near misses, the people like Eric Clapton, Iggy Pop and Keith Richard, who have drifted into varying degrees of addiction and then come out of it the hard way, still represent a loss to sum total music in terms of what they didn't produce during their periods of dependency.

It's not only overdose and addiction that

Bob Marley — prophet of Jah, burnin' and a-lootin' and a-smokin' ganja.

George Snow

cause the drug problems in rock and roll. Another lurking temptation, particularly when hard times hit a band, is to get into a bit of dealing to boost a flagging income. These adventures in illicit free enterprise can all too often end in arrest, scandal and a stretch in the slammers.

One such case is Wayne Kramer, one time guitar player with the MC5, the Detroit high energy band. The mid-seventies hadn't been altogether too successful for Kramer. Like many other Detroit musicians, he had felt the pinch of the recession that hit the city's auto based economy in the wake of the energy crisis. When, one night in a club, he was asked if he could obtain a small amount of cocaine, he reluctantly agreed. The lure of the few bucks that could be made on the deal outweighed his natural caution.

Over the next eight months, the small people came back to Kramer. The requests for him to score some coke for them became more frequent, the amounts involved and the sums changing hands grew increasingly larger.

This period of affluence ended in a spectacular raid on Kramer's Detroit apartment. To his horror he discovered the people he'd been doing business with were Drug Enforcement Agency operatives. During their

Jim Croce, another rock airwreck victim

eight month association with Kramer, the DEA men had been building up a dossier that was to be the basis of the prosecution evidence at his trial.

Kramer was sentenced to five years by a judge who rejected all testimony that referred to Kramer's talent, reputation and career prospects.

It's very easy to look for an external explanation for problems that occur in any walk of life. It's very easy for the rock business to turn round and look at its casualties and say 'Oh yeah, it was the drugs' or 'He was always a fuck-up anyway'. There's a tendency never to blame the disasters of the rock and roll business on the rock and roll business itself.

If you take them one stage beyond the superficials, there's little doubt that the pressure of sudden success, previously unimagined amounts of money, and instant notoriety, is frequently more than the individual, particularly an individual in or just out of his teens, can take.

Just because that same individual has proficiency on an instrument, a good voice or a pretty face, it doesn't guarantee that his personality is the kind that can stand up to the pressure created by high speed fame or, much more important, the ever present knowledge that the fame can be whisked away as fast as it came.

Going on can be just as much of an ordeal as getting there. Holding on to success can be as much of a trial as achieving it in the first place. Pete Townshend summed up this feeling. He was talking about the Who's early days of mayhem and guitar smashing.

'There were times when it seemed as though there was nowhere else to go. I felt that all we could do was strap dynamite all over our bodies and blow up the club, the audience and ourselves.'

Although few other musicians have articulated this state of mind with such dramatic clarity, the feeling isn't uncommon. Rock and roll is a business where the maxim that 'you're only as good as your last record' is invoked with a vengeance. Bearing this in mind, it's little wonder that too many performers retreat, by one means or another, into some kind of fantasy world. It's in this retreat that the music claims the majority of its victims■

7

National Westminster B

Chelsea, Old Church Branch
30 King's Road, Chelsea, London SW3

Pay  *Slush Fund*

JUST ONE THIN DIME

BRADBURY, WILKINSON & Cº Lº NEW MALDEN.

⑆899652⑆ 60⑈0515⑉

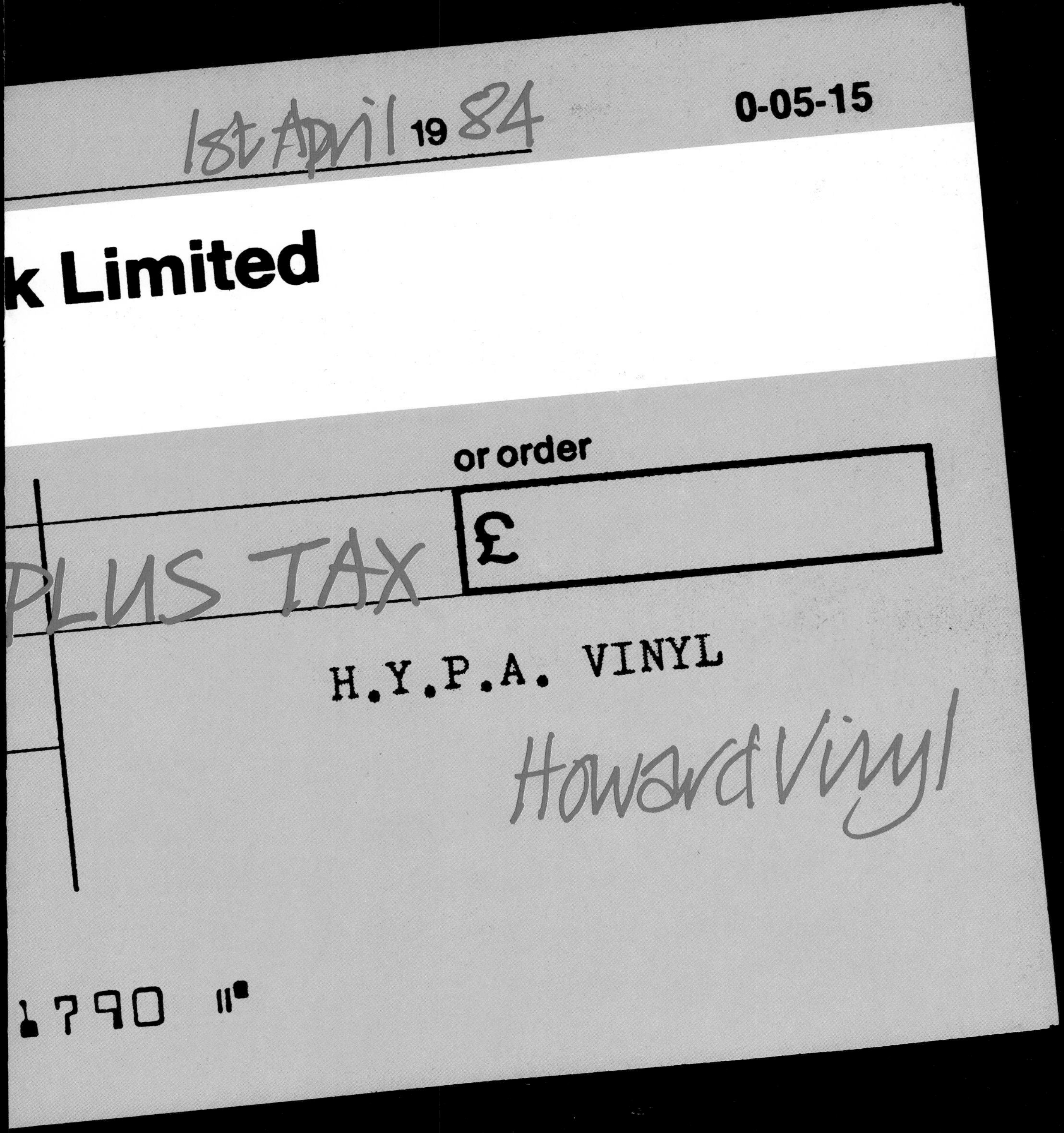

1st April 19 84

0-05-15

k Limited

or order

PLUS TAX

£

H.Y.P.A. VINYL

Howard Vinyl

1790 ıı

JUST AS EVERY fairground has its barkers to sucker in the rubes, rock and roll has its own pitch men to bring the people to the music. It takes a lot more than an individual with strong lungs to satisfy the needs of the rock industry, but in the end the results are the same. The rock promo man may talk about grosses, units and product instead of selling to to the suckers, but in a lot of ways he means pretty much the same thing. He has to convince the passing public that rock and roll can't live without the wonderful new record by blah blah.

The rock business takes its promotion very seriously. The promo department of any record company is virtually an industry within an industry. It produces badges, T-shirts, bowling jackets, belt buckles, balloons, wristwatches, toys, lighters and acres upon acres of print, all dedicated to the greater glory of one or another of the company's acts.

There have been times when management or record company promotional campaigns have become so lavish that they have almost eclipsed the music they were supposed to be selling. In a business which is ultra prone to wallowing in excess, the promotion end is no exception.

At root, the name of the game is to sell records. This is, for everyone concerned, where the real money lies. Bands may earn their bread and butter by playing live dates, but it's record sales that transform that bread and butter into the million dollar club sandwich which, if the truth were told, is the goal of just about every rock and roller.

The cliche about nothing succeeding like success is nowhere more true than in the music industry. Thousands of dollars a week are spent making sure that success is instantly and accurately catalogued. This cataloguing is what is commonly known as the charts. Week in and week out, the top thirty, fifty or hundred are diligently studied by the musicians, the businessmen and the customers.

For the musician, a chart placing is the open door to TV, radio, better dates and pictures in the newspapers. For the business it's the herald of cash in the bank. For the customer it's an indication of what everyone else across the country is buying and listening to. All too often, if sufficient people buy a record, a whole lot more are going to follow suit.

The charts have become a sales guide that actually generates more sales. In order to make a place in the charts a record not only has to sell in quantity, it has to sell fast.

If a record manages to sell maybe one hundred thousand units in a week, it will, because of the charts, appear to be far more successful than another record that sells exactly the same amount over a longer period.

This need to move records at high speed has made the promotion and publicity departments crucial to the record companies. A campaign has to be timed so that as far as is possible, a general desire to buy the record has been created before it is even available in the shops.

Moira Bellas is director of publicity for WEA Records in the UK. Her job is to ensure that any record released by artists under contract to the company receives the maximum possible press coverage.

This is only one part, however, of the full, multiple thrust promotion campaign. In addition to the press office, there are the pluggers who attempt to persuade the discjockeys to play the record, and the promotion department, which is responsible for posters, billboards, point of sale display and all paid advertising.

One of the main projects for WEA during the late summer of 1977 was the release campaign for the double Rolling Stones album *Love You Live*. In some ways this was not a typical publicity thrust. Normally there's little difficulty in getting the press and public to notice a brand new Stones album. There were a few problems to overcome, though.

Love You Live was the last album the Stones would be making for WEA. They had already signed a four record deal with the rival EMI corporation. In addition to this, the rock and roll rumour mill had decided that the Stones were slipping. Their recorded output had become noticeably thin over the previous couple of years and, just to make things worse, there had been a lot of less than complimentary press about Mick Jagger's marriage and Keith Richard's drugs problem.

The event of the new wave hadn't helped either. Bands like the Sex Pistols were apparently eroding the Stones' traditional

**Press kit for the Rolling Stones
'Love You Live' album**

outlaw thunder.

It was decided that the campaign for the new record should be a long, careful exercise.

'The first move was when Earl McGrath, who runs Rolling Stones Records in the USA, brought me the cover artwork for the album. He said that Mick was going to be in town and that we should have a meeting to discuss the promotion of the album,' Moira explains.

This meeting would involve all areas of the company's selling force. This was two months before the proposed release date.

'We all put forward our various ideas. What money was going to be spent on advertising, where it was going to be spent.'

Two days later there was a press and promotion meeting that took things a stage further.

'Obviously Mick Jagger was very positive about the press and promotion side. From my point of view, it was the first time I'd sat in on a meeting with Mick Jagger to discuss the promotion of a Rolling Stones album. It was pretty nerve-racking for me. I went in fully armed with ideas. I heard he was the sort of person who liked creative people and if you just sat there coming out with routine moves

he wouldn't tolerate it for long.

'I wanted to drop the idea of a lavish party. As the album was live I wanted to do something where the album was simply played. I wanted this done at a live venue, just to get across the idea that it was a very good live album. We chose the Marquee Club because it was one of the places where the Stones had first played.

'My original idea that actually didn't work, in the end, was to have lots of film from all through the Stones' career, stuff with Brian Jones in, all jumbled together playing non-stop on TV screens round the room, giving a really live feel.

'Everyone goes to a Stones party and they expect cuckoos to come out of the wall and clowns to jump up in the air. I wanted to drop all that and concentrate on the album. I think if we'd done anything else the Stones would have been ripped apart for being flash in this day and age when times are hard.'

In addition to the party, Moira Bellas' group also turned out a press kit. The press kit is an important aid to the publicity end of any campaign. It's the press kit's function to catch the imagination of journalists and, with luck, get them to listen to the record with some degree of sympathy.

In the case of this Stones campaign the press kit, like the party, was a fairly low-key object. Its theme was a somewhat bizarre series of photographs of the band biting each other. They were reproduced in press ads, on posters, and incorporated in the cover. The album arrived at the various newspapers in a simple brown paper carrier-bag. With it came another set of the pictures, a poster and a set of rubber lips.

Toys of this kind, although frivolous on the surface, do have a logical function. They can frequently spark off a bout of newspaper office horseplay that can't help but draw attention to the record.

The rubber lips were particularly success-ful. More than one office buffoon put them on and started doing bad Jagger imperson-ations.

The biting pictures were similarly successful. The week after the release of the Stones album, pictures began to appear of other, less well-known bands busily chewing on each other in parody of the Stones. They may have been promoting themselves but, at the same time, they drew attention back to the original campaign.

The Stones promotion had been kept fairly low-key, in this instance. Other sales pushes have been pitched on a much more lavish scale. Some campaigns have even gone down in the unofficial history of rock and roll.

In 1969, the managers of an unknown British band, Brinsley Schwarz, spent a not inconsiderable fortune jetting an entire plane load of British journalists from London to New York to see the group play at the then prestigious Fillmore East.

This was a case where promotion serious-ly backfired. The concert was a fiasco, and it took the band a full five years to live down the reputation they'd gained as being a talentless hype.

There are times when throwing money about like confetti can actually aid a band. When Alice Cooper was making his first major European breakthrough, his promo people rented a suburban zoo and funfair just outside London and filled it with press, personalities, music business hustlers, disc-jockeys and freaks. Midgets, clowns and strippers were

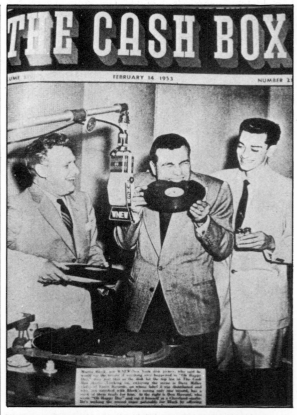

Alan Freed was run out rock & roll after a fifties pa ola scandal, proving that mus is bad for the digestion.

Janie Jones added prostituti to payola and wound up in ja

ice Cooper was undoubtedly
e major promotion epic
til . . .

hired to provide a non-stop, decadent spectacle. The whole thing was topped with unlimited booze and the result turned out to be one of the more outrageous, drunken orgies of rock promotion history.

A British MP felt Cooper ought to be deported. The press lavished every attention on him, and the band moved from being minority interest weirdos to a headline act.

Despite a lot of popular speculation, bribery hardly ever plays a part in rock and roll promotion. Over the years there have been scandals. The most notable was in the late fifties when Alan Freed, the DJ who claimed to have originally coined the phrase rock and roll, was hounded out of business after he'd been accused of accepting payola.

Payola rumours have erupted at other times. A certain soul band was reputed to lay on hookers and cocaine to enlist the sympathey of press and radio people. In London, singer Janie Jones was jailed for six years on prostitution charges after the press unearthed the story of a call-girl service operating for the benefit of better relationships between record pluggers and disc-jockeys.

In the main though, these incidents are the exception rather than the rule. There may be times when promo gifts run a little close to the bribe level. The five dollar give-away T-shirt may escalate to a fifty dollar jacket or a hundred dollar wristwatch. Generally, although they are universally well received, these do little directly to influence the opinions of the lucky recipient.

On the surface, a lot of rock promotion may seem trivial and frivolous. People have said the same thing about other kinds of advertising. It isn't that easy to dismiss an operation that annually turns over millions of dollars.

One of the most successful promotions in rock and roll has to be for the band Kiss. In an amazingly short space of time, what really amounted to a no better than average heavy metal outfit was transformed into one of America's biggest cult bands.

The brain behind this transformation was Bill Aucoin. In his office on Madison Avenue are four puppet figures of his golden band. Although everyone in the Aucoin organisation tells you the members of the band are anything but the puppets of their manager, it seems strangely significant.

... Kiss

their live album *Kiss Alive* went gold, then platinum, then double platinum. The two subsequent albums, *Destroyer* and *Rock and Roll Over* followed it into the million-plus units bracket.

This deluge of bucks really enabled Kiss to extend their fantasy to almost unreal extremes. They went in for fire-eating and equipped themselves with one of the biggest touring stages that have ever been used in rock and roll. It came complete with a ruined castle for blood spitting bass player Gene Simmons, huge demon cat statues and levitating drums.

This dizzy pinnacle of success wasn't reached without a good deal of sweat and tears (as well as the aforementioned blood).

Aucoin promoted Kiss in complete reversal of the usual techniques. He kept the band almost totally under wraps for many months after he took over their management. All that the media was allowed to see was the fully made-up stage personae of the band.

Even today, the image making process dictates that photographers must sign clearances which specify that they will on no account take pictures of the band without their stage make-up. This policy has been strictly adhered to and, up to now, nobody has yet seen the naked faces of Kiss.

This risky form of promotion seems to have paid off in a massive way. Kiss now has a huge following both in the USA and Japan. Somehow they have created a kind of cardboard cutout air of gothic mystery around themselves that appeals to thousands upon thousands of kids' morbid fantasies.

Bill Aucoin ran into Kiss in early 1974. He was running an independent TV production company that put out a syndicated rock show called Flipside. Kiss was a struggling rock combo, very involved in heavy metal, heavy theatre and heavy make-up.

When promoters wouldn't book them they rented halls in order to put on their own shows.

Aucoin spotted the band at one of these self-help gigs, and told them that he wanted to manage them. His offer was unique. If he couldn't get them a recording contract in two weeks, both parties would go their separate ways.

Aucoin hit his goal with a couple of days to spare, signing Kiss to Neil Bogart's Casablanca label. Despite this initial energy burst, it was hardly a case of overnight success. Kiss and Aucoin made three albums, struggled through a series of tours, often financed on the brink of collapse by Aucoin's American Express card.

They were jumped on by any critic who could spell 'moronic' or 'cretinous' and wound up several hundred thousand dollars in debt.

Almost impossibly, Kiss and Aucoin stayed with it. They neither altered the music nor the make-up. Just when it seemed as though there was nothing to do but give up,

Their success is no longer confined to rock and roll, either. In the summer of 1977 the Marvel Comics Group, inventors of *Doctor Strange* and *Captain America*, published the first issue of a Kiss fantasy comic in which the band was transformed into full blown superheroes. Simultaneously the band was working on a full length feature movie in a similar vein. Bill Aucoin sums up:

'It's escapism. The kids who come and watch Kiss are working out their fantasies. That's what the band's saying. Be what you want to be, just like we're doing.'

Unfortunately, it appears that far too many of the kids simply want to be carbon copies of Kiss, but that's often the way it goes in rock and roll■

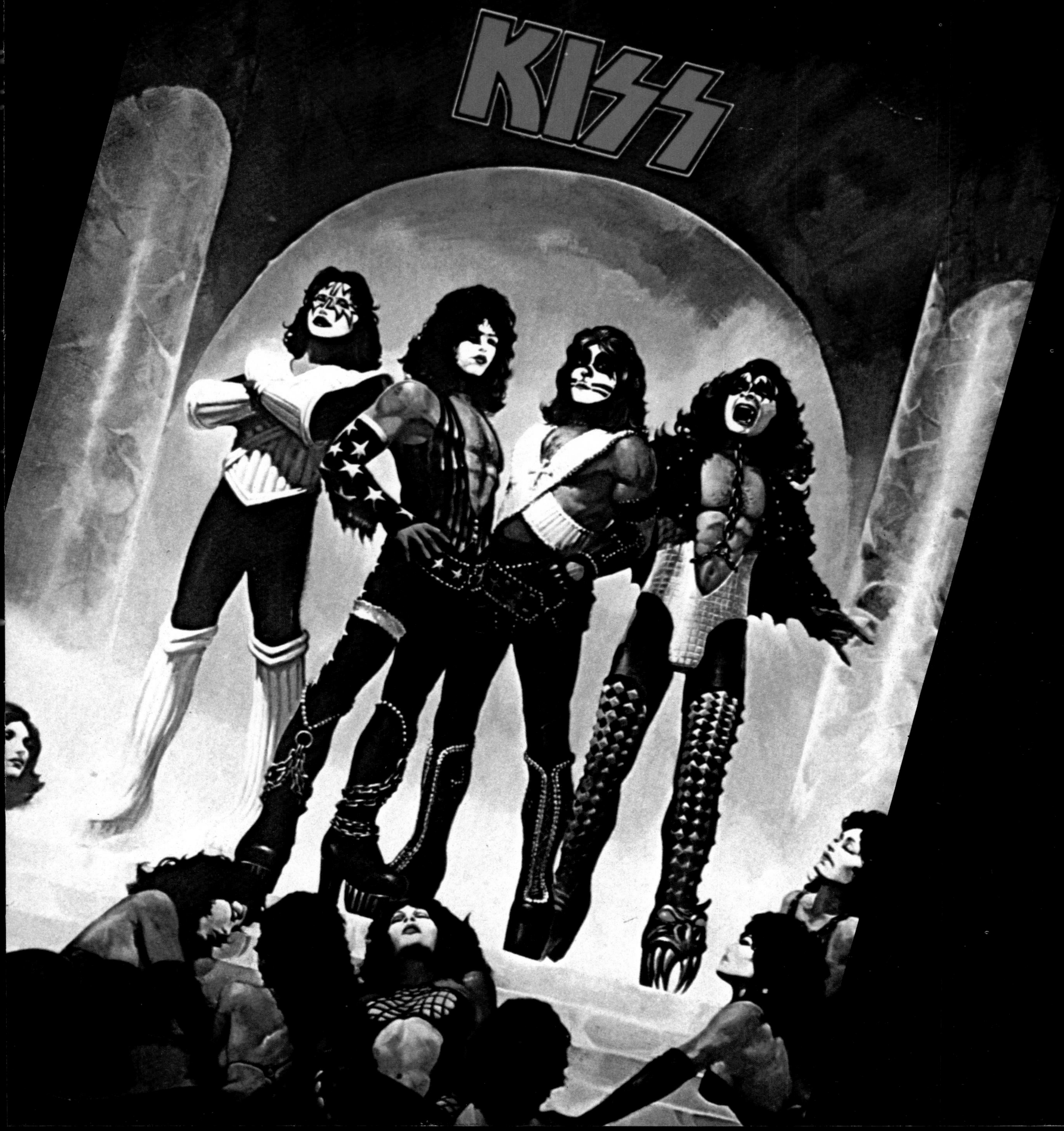
KISS

Nowhere To Go But Down

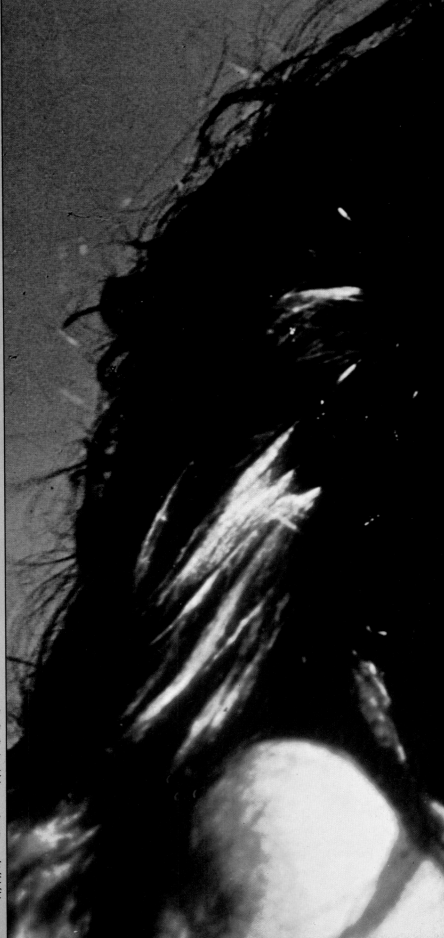

BILL GRAHAM has often repeated the question: 'What does an individual do when he reaches the top and still doesn't find any real satisfaction?' He says 'Anyone who's down, who's a failure or who's still trying to make it can tell themselves that they are unhappy because they aren't successful. If you've reached the very peak of your career, and you still aren't happy, you can't use that excuse. The source of your unhappiness is within yourself, and that's one hell of a hard thing to face.'

It's all too possible, in rock and roll, for someone who's hardly had any experience of life to be precipitated into a position of

adopted two very different paths for coping with their almost impossible position in the rock and roll pantheon.

Success for the Stones was a simple, one-way street to fame and fortune. Their unique role as the bad boys of music in the 1960s caused authority to take them all too seriously, and the heat came down in the form of a series of narcotics busts. In 1967 the establishment, personified by a provincial British judge, came close to nailing the two prime Stones to the wall, when sentences of three and twelve months were handed down on Jagger and Richard.

Although the resulting public outcry saved them from anything more than a couple of days in the slammers, it served to ram home the message that even top rock stars could be up for grabs, the same as anyone else.

The same lesson was reinforced two years later, by the Stones' own peer group after the Hell's Angels' rampage at the Altamont free concert. The consensus of opinion was that the Stones had simply gone too far with their fantasy of being satanic princelings. A fantasy was okay, as long as it didn't cost lives. It was not only the death of Meredith Hunter but also the fact that he was apparently pointing a gun at Jagger when the Hell's Angels cut him down, that really shocked the rock and roll world.

Altamont, in many ways, was a turning point for the Stones. Both Jagger and Richard appeared to retreat slightly afterwards. They

'Sweet Gene Vincent' — gammy leg but nimble finger Bob Dylan — what can I say Keith Richard — nowhere go but down, and in a roun about way.

unbelievable success. One day they're nobody, the next, the devil seems to be laying out all the countries of the earth in front of them. It has snapped more than one mind. From these high places of rock and roll there's really no way to go but down.

This is the ultimate high wire act in the rock and roll circus. All too frequently it lasts for life.

Different individuals have reacted to the sudden onslaught of rock success in different ways. Jimi Hendrix and Janis Joplin were swamped by the wave. Others, like Brian Wilson of the Beach Boys, have retreated into therapy, occasional psychosis and bouts of drug taking.

The two leading figures in the Rolling Stones, Mick Jagger and Keith Richard, have

has made himself, probably very consciously, into such an engima that literally millions of words have been churned out speculating on the motives and hidden meanings, real or imagined, behind his songs.

Dylan has always had a unique ability to switch images at exactly the right time to keep his fans confused and guessing. During his early days in New York he presented himself as the wandering punk-of-the-earth, a Woody Guthrie of the sixties, fresh out of the Midwest.

No sooner had be been accepted by the folk protest movement as its boy-hero, than he quickly threw off the mantle of commitment and emerged transformed as a caustic, Rimbaud-based poet. He was turning out the most surreal images that rock and roll had ever seen by day, and holding court in the cafes and bars of Greenwich Village by night, waiting to be presented with victims for his vicious wit.

The phase continued in even more convoluted form until he fell head first off his motorcycle in mid-1966. The motorcycle accident was a blessing in disguise. The frenzy that surrounded Dylan had risen to such a peak that people were talking about him in terms of a messiah, and Dylan was reportedly getting paranoid about the possibility of being assassinated.

The period of convalescence after the crash in which, incidentally, he broke his neck, led into an extended period of Garbo-like isolation. Critics viewed phrases like 'No

modified their images. Jagger married and started to run with the international jet set. It was almost as though he was looking for traditional, elitist protection.

Keith Richard, on the other hand, took his step back in an altogether different manner. More and more he seemed set on a course of very elegant but very definite self-destruction. The end product of this languid pose was heroin addiction. This in its turn led to the gates of a Canadian prison.

The Stones' retreat from the problems of massive rock and roll stardom started from incidents like Altamont and their drug busts. Bob Dylan, on the other hand, has twisted and turned, alternately revealing and concealing himself to his public, almost from the very start of his career. In fact, Dylan

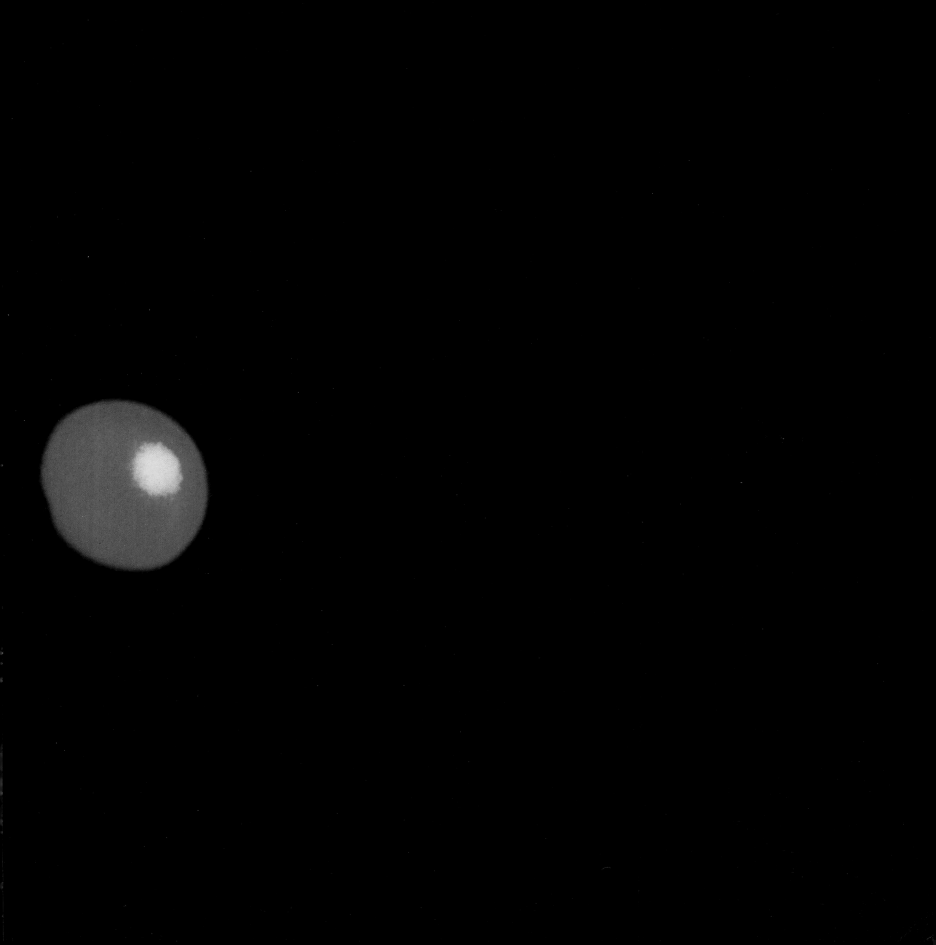

martyr is among you now that you can call your own' from his *John Wesley Harding* album as a definite farewell to his previous life and the attitudes of his followers.

Certainly the long stretch of rural retreat, from which he only ventured out to flirt with Johnny Cash and the downhome world of country music, tended to confirm this.

Just as the world had started to write off Dylan as a hopeless hermit, he suddenly reappeared with the Band in a storming 1974 tour of the USA. The ticket applications for the tour reportedly totalled some six million.

After the tour there was the album *Blood on the Tracks*, which was hailed as Dylan's masterpiece of the seventies. Dylan was back with a vengeance, right at the time when the music business was gearing up to write him off.

As if these achievements weren't enough, 1976 once again saw Dylan on the move, this time with the pioneering Rolling Thunder Revue.

Rolling Thunder was a typical Dylan move. The normal big league rock and roll tour had by that time become something of a juggernaut that did more to separate performer and audience than bring them together. Dylan totally rejected this concept

Bob Dylan's Rolling Thunder Review attempted to establish a more human approach to rock & roll touring, both for performers and audience.

and instead, in a number of all-night sessions in New York's Gramercy Park Hotel, he hatched an entirely different scheme.

Dylan's concept was typically free-form, revolutionarily so in a rock industry which had reached a peak of rigid formalization. He basically wanted to play small clubs. In order to do this he was to hit the road with a pick-up band, including ex-David Bowie sideman

Mick Ronson plus a large, assorted roster of guests. It seemed closer to a traditional ragbag passing show than anything rock and roll had seen for decades.

In the beginning Rolling Thunder did exactly what was intended. It stuck to small

clubs and campus halls across the American north east. Even Dylan, however, couldn't deny his popularity for long. In its second phase, the scale of Rolling Thunder began to escalate until it had built up to a massive open air concert at Fort Collins, Colorado, which was filmed by CBS Television and put out on the network under the title *Hard Rain*. Rolling Thunder may not have stuck consistently to its original dream, but it did amply demonstrate to an over-organized rock world that there was still room for originality in the presentation of live music. The task didn't necessarily entail massive banks of lasers, NASA scale technology and a road crew big enough to build pyramids.

It would be foolish to assume that Bob Dylan has come through nearly a decade and a half of superstardom and stayed mentally unscathed. He was put in a position by his fans, particularly during the sixties, where he was virtually used by a whole generation as a substitute conscience.

What does stand out is that Dylan's chameleon-like changes of image and intense

protection of areas of his private life have brought him through the rigours of world fame in much better shape than others who have shared the experience.

Certainly a comparison between Dylan and Elvis Presley indicates something of the kind.

I doubt that anyone reading this book needs to be reminded that the figure of Elvis Presley towered over all other rock stars who followed him. His incredible success·is now a matter of well-documented history. So is the way his success got so out of hand. For ten years he refused to perform in public and retreated behind the high, guarded walls and locked gates of his Los Angeles and Memphis mansions. For ten years after Presley's discharge from the army, his only contact with his vast, global public was a series of increasingly depressing, truly awful films. During all this time, it looked as though all information that filtered through to Presley was thoroughly processed by his manager, Colonel Tom Parker, his producer, Felton Jarvis and his payrolled boyhood buddies, the so-called Memphis Mafia.

At the start of the seventies it looked as if Presley might be coming out of his isolation and making something of an artistic comeback. Singles like *Guitar Man* and *Burning Love* were among his best work since the classic recordings of the fifties. He started appearing live again, even if it was in the slightly unreal

For too many of his fans, the decline of Elvis Presley was slow process of erosion and decay of an incredible talent yet, surprisingly, millions of them remained fanatically loyal.

world of the big Las Vegas lounges.

The comeback didn't last however. It was over almost as soon as it had started. Stories began to circulate in the Hollywood gossip magazines about how Presley was becoming mentally unstable. He had apparently become a compulsive eater. Gradually Presley turned into an obese wreck whose stage shows moved him nearer and nearer to disaster.

These were the superficials of the Elvis Presley story. Everyone knew that the dynamic idol of millions had lapsed into flabby middle age. The world had seen how it had happened, but nobody, except the closed Presley inner circle, knew why it had happened.

What actually went on inside the Presley mansions was a carefully guarded mystery. At least it was up to June 1976 when, in an apparent fit of pique, Elvis fired three body-guards, Red West, Sonny West and Dave Hebler, who had been with him through most of his career. They went to the press and, as inner ring members of the Memphis Mafia, they were in a position to give amazing, and often alarming, insights into what it really meant to be Elvis Presley.

Although the revelations presented by Hebler and the two West cousins were pitched on the most gosh-wow sensational level, a clear picture does emerge of a completely cut off Presley, slowly regressing into a totally

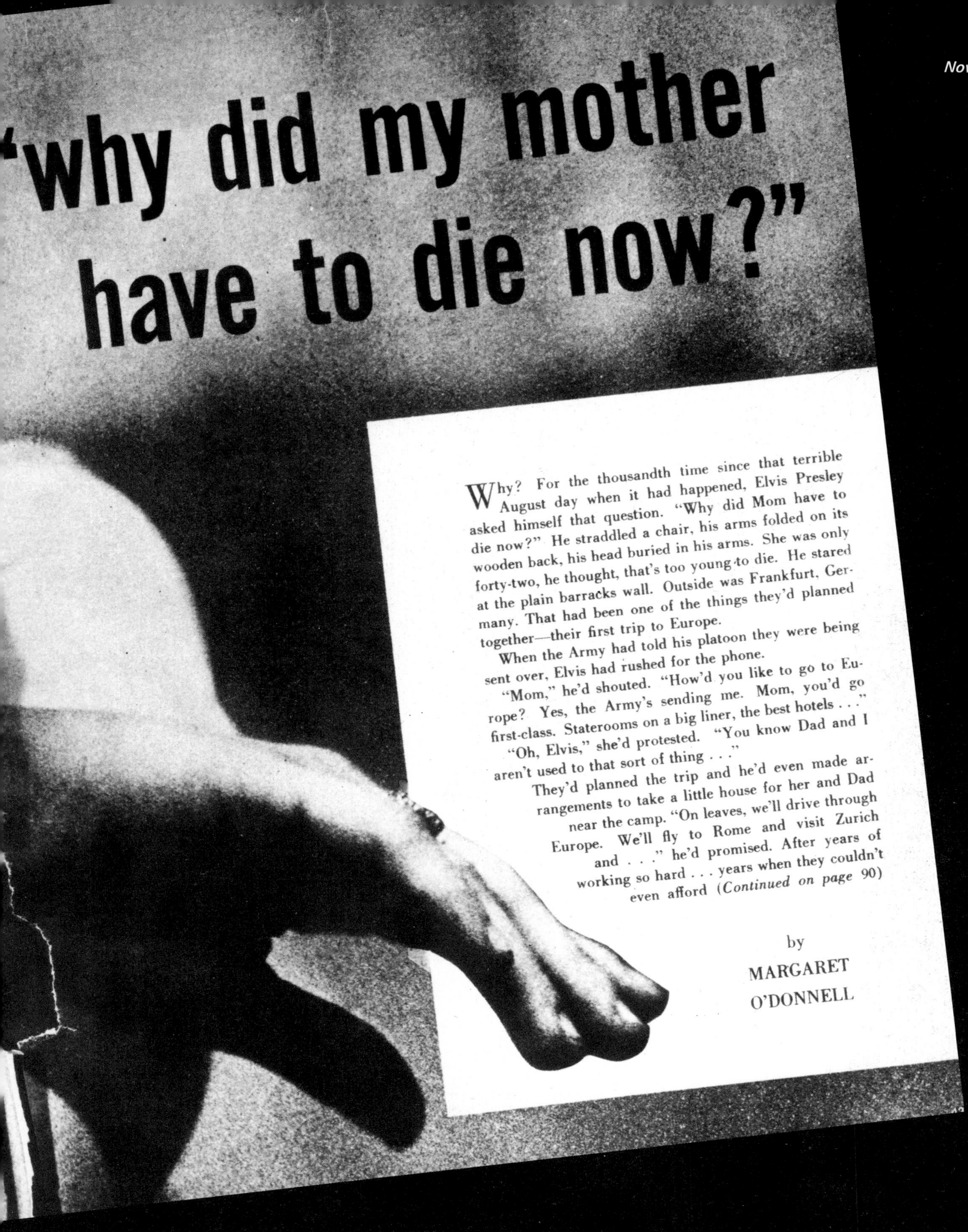

"why did my mother have to die now?"

Why? For the thousandth time since that terrible August day when it had happened, Elvis Presley asked himself that question. "Why did Mom have to die now?" He straddled a chair, his arms folded on its wooden back, his head buried in his arms. She was only forty-two, he thought, that's too young to die. He stared at the plain barracks wall. Outside was Frankfurt, Germany. That had been one of the things they'd planned together—their first trip to Europe.

When the Army had told his platoon they were being sent over, Elvis had rushed for the phone.

"Mom," he'd shouted. "How'd you like to go to Europe? Yes, the Army's sending me. Mom, you'd go first-class. Staterooms on a big liner, the best hotels . . ."

"Oh, Elvis," she'd protested. "You know Dad and I aren't used to that sort of thing . . ."

They'd planned the trip and he'd even made arrangements to take a little house for her and Dad near the camp. "On leaves, we'll drive through Europe. We'll fly to Rome and visit Zurich and . . ." he'd promised. After years of working so hard . . . years when they couldn't even afford (Continued on page 90)

by

MARGARET
O'DONNELL

irresponsible, grossly pampered infant who would tolerate no restraints on his behaviour.

The far from heroic portrait of Presley painted by his three ex-bodyguards shows a man who felt he could get away with anything. Women moved through his life with such speed and in such numbers that you could easily imagine them being delivered to his door in packs of six, along with the milk. In addition to this almost pathological need for instant and continual sex, Presley was reported to be dependent on massive cocktails of various pills, both uppers and downers, to keep his metabolism level.

Twenty years of being the ultimate superstar, according to West, West and Hebler, also left Presley with a regard for his own importance that almost rivalled that of a banana republic tyrant.

He expressed the opinion that his hands held the power of healing and, if he bothered to concentrate hard enough, he would be able to change the weather and even maybe affect the course of world events.

He could not tolerate being denied even his slightest whim. His usually salaried companions had to be on twenty-four hour call to indulge him. It was not uncommon for Presley suddenly to decide he wanted to shoot pool at 4 a.m. or to shoot out a TV set when he disliked the programme.

His tantrums when he couldn't get his own way were allegedly awesome. On more than one occasion he threatened Red West with a gun when the faithful retainer had displeased him in some way. He also injured a young woman with a pool cue when she interrupted one of his games.

Probably the most outlandish of Elvis Presley's excesses was when he attempted to arrange a murder contract on Mike Stone, the karate instructor who took away his wife Priscilla.

As Sonny West tells it, Presley came to him on the edge of hysteria and told him:

'The man has to die. You know the man has to die. The son of a bitch must go. You know it, Sonny. You know it. There is so much pain in me, and he did it. Do you hear me? I am right. You know I'm right. Mike Stone has to die. You will do it for me. Kill the son of a bitch.'

After this speech Presley literally attempted to climb the wall. The bodyguards hoped the idea of murder might fade with time. Unfortunately it didn't and, reluctantly, Red West searched out a possible hit man. The going rate was ten thousand dollars.

When confronted with the final decision Presley backed away from the killing.

'Aw, hell. Let's leave it for now. Maybe it's a bit heavy.'

This was possibly the first time in many years that Elvis Presley had come face to face with reality, and it took the brink of a conspiracy to murder to bring him to it. Up to that point he was behaving with the paranoid lack of awareness of a psychotic dictator or mafia chieftain.

The final act in the Presley saga ended on 16 August 1977 when he collapsed in his luxury Memphis home. Although the official cause of death was recorded as a heart attack, it is almost certain that what really killed Elvis Presley was the incredible isolation that stardom imposed on him.

He died, lonely and disturbed, in the Memphis mansion that had become a virtual prison.

The news of his death drove everything else off the front pages of the newspapers and the lead slots of the TV news shows. His funeral was a point of pilgrimage for tens of thousands of fans. Two million Presley records were sold within twenty-four hours of his death. The worldwide grief elevated the Presley legend until it was bigger than anything that had gone before. It was unfortunately too late to save the man. At the end, Presley had no one prepared to stand up to him or tell him that he was screwing up.

Perhaps this is the ultimate lesson of both rock and roll and instant stardom. The acclaim that the successful musician is subjected to can frequently warp his or her mind. The greater the fame, the greater the difficulty in staying in touch with the real world. Maybe if the ascent to the dizzy heights went more slowly, the individual would have a chance to mature as a human being before life's normal reference points were removed from his grasp.

As it is, the rise to fame is still, more often than not, meteoric, and the descent is usually wretched. Maybe it's the minus side of the whole show, maybe it's the major danger to the music. One thing's for sure, it's not likely to change in a hurry ∎

The Who — after one US tour Keith Moon came home with £73 profit. Vandalism doesn't pay.

ONE THING'S FOR sure, rock and roll isn't going to go away in the foreseeable future. Despite all the predictions that the music was going to be dead inside of six months, it has grown, proliferated and diversified over the last twenty years to the point where it has outstripped every other form of music in popularity.

While it still has the ability to mutate, rock will remain a vital and healthy art form. It seems that just as one generation of rockers start to grow fat (either spiritually or physically) and complacent, another generation shows up to carry on the tradition.

Right at this moment the industry is reeling under the impact of the punk/new wave phenomenon. Although veterans of the endless highway may complain that the punks are only grabbing one per cent of the audience, half a per cent of the record sales and ninety per cent of the press coverage, it's unlikely that they'll go away.

The punks are in the direct tradition of all good rock music. They are kids playing for their own peer group. Whether they are the future of rock remains to be seen. What we can be certain of is that rock has a very positive future.

"In 1977 rock has become a gladiatorial sport" — Jean-Jacques Burnel of the Stranglers